13/7/5.

Caring Moments:
The discourse of reflective practice

FOR
REFERENCE ONLY

Other titles in the series

- *Reflection: Principles and practice for healthcare professionals* by Tony Ghaye and Sue Lillyman

- *Effective Clinical Supervision: The role of reflection* edited by Tony Ghaye and Sue Lillyman

- *Empowerment through Reflection: The narratives of healthcare professionals* edited by Tony Ghaye, Dave Gillespie and Sue Lillyman

- *The Reflective Mentor* by Tony Ghaye and Sue Lillyman

Caring Moments:
The discourse of reflective practice

edited by

Tony Ghaye and Sue Lillyman

Quay
Books

Mark Allen
Publishing Ltd

Quay Books, Mark Allen Publishing Ltd
Jesses Farm, Snow Hill, Dinton, Wiltshire, SP3 5HN

British Library Cataloguing-in-Publication Data
A catalogue record is available for this book

© Mark Allen Publishing Ltd 2000
ISBN 1 85642 126 0

Printed in the UK by The Cromwell Press, Trowbridge, Wiltshire

Contents

About the contributors

Val Chapman PhD, MSc, Cert Ed, DIP RSA (SpLD)
*Equal Opportunities Co-ordinator, University College
Worcester*

I am the Equal Opportunities Co-ordinator at University College
Worcester where I also lecture within the Faculty of Education and
Psychology. I have taught in various higher education institutions in
the UK and abroad (including Nigeria, Japan and Hong Kong) as
well as across all age phases within schools and have served as a
Local Education Authority Advisory Teacher. Although originally
training as a physical education specialist, I have particular interest
and experience in the area of Specific Learning Difficulties within
the broader area of SEN. My completed doctoral research focused on
the area of dyspraxia.

Tony Ghaye Cert Educ, BEd (Hons), MA (Educ), PhD
*Professor of Education and Director of The Policy into
Practice Research Centre, University College Worcester*

In my working life I have been fortunate in being able to work with
and learn from a very wide range of professionals, such as GPs,
social workers, police and probation officers, therapists of various
kinds, osteopaths and school teachers. I have also had the privilege
and challenge of working with individuals and communities in the
Third World and in emerging nations in North Africa and the Middle
East. This experience has energised my commitment to inter-
professional learning and multi-disciplinary working to help to
improve what we do with and for others. I see reflective practice and
action research as a central part of my work. I have just completed
the largest survey of its kind undertaken in the UK into young
people's attitude towards and behaviour in relation to illicit drugs
and alcohol. This contributed to improvements in service policy and
practice. I am the founder and Editor-in-Chief of the new multi-
disciplinary international Carfax journal called *Reflective Practice*,
which published its first issue in March 2000.

Josephine Hamilton-Jones BSc (Hons), Tech, PhD
Senior Lecturer in IT and Computer Modelling, University College Worcester

I grew up in Sheffield, South Yorkshire in an academic, music and sports orientated environment. I gained a degree in Mathematics and its Applications at University of Wales Institute of Science and Technology, Cardiff in 1983 and completed my doctorate in 1987, considering the strategies used to solve battle equations and employing these methods to solve equations in epidemiology. With a young family, I moved into further education and lectured in mathematics, computing and information technology at several colleges around the country, rising to management level. Since 1994, I have been an examiner, mentor and tutor in quantitative methods for the National Extension College to home and international students studying degrees through distance learning.

I returned to Higher Education in 1997 to pursue my research interests in simulation, modelling and the use of IT for teaching and learning. I lecture in Information Technology and Computer Modelling at University College Worcester.

Ruth Hardie RGN
Matron, St Mary Stevens Hospice, Oldwinford, West Midlands

Since qualifying in 1985 I have gained a wide range of nursing experience in a variety of fields. I am currently Matron of a Hospice believing, in my role, that there needs to be strong nursing leadership to empower my staff to give high quality nursing care. I am undertaking an MSc at University College Worcester. My interests are in critical reflective practice, effective communication, patient autonomy and interdisciplinary team work, maintaining that you need all of these aspects to ensure that patients receive the most appropriate care and staff reach their full potential.

Sue Lillyman MA, BSc (Nursing), RGN, RM, DPSN, PGCE (FAHE)
Faculty Head of Quality Assurance, University of Central England, Faculty of Health and Community Care

Having qualified as a Registered General Nurse in 1980 and Midwife in 1983 I worked within various areas, including intensive care, gynaecology and care of the elderly, rehabilitation and acute medicine until entering nurse education in 1989. Having transferred with the Colleges of Nursing into the University of Central England I worked as a Senior Lecturer within the Personal Development Unit for the Faculty of Health and Community Care and in 1997 took up my current role as Faculty Head of Quality Assurance. My teaching responsibilities have been with post registration nurses undertaking diploma, degree and masters courses in nursing and collaborative community care masters course for healthcare workers. Specialist areas of interest include, care of the elderly, reflective practice, competence in practice, critical thinking and professional issues.

Sarah Mann RGN, BSc (Hons)
Senior Staff Nurse, Endoscopy, Redditch

I have been employed as Senior Staff Nurse on the Endoscopy Unit at the Alexandra Hospital in Redditch for eighteen months. Prior to this I worked for eighteen months on Endoscopy at Heartlands Hospital in Birmingham. My present post involves the provision of both therapeutic and diagnostic gastroscopy, colonoscopy, broncho-scopy and ERCP for both in and outpatients. The work involves the physical and psychological preparation of patients, providing assistance to the medical staff and the recovery and advising of patients before discharge. I am involved in the day-to-day management of the unit, ensuring the smooth running of the lists and planning for unscheduled procedures. My interest in training and teaching has enabled me to develop an in-house training plan for use on the endoscopy unit and to be actively involved in the training of staff new to the unit. I find the post a challenging one and hope to be able to develop my role of nurse, manager and teacher.

Helen Taylor BSc (Hons) Nursing, PGCE, RGN

I read for a degree in nursing at Leeds Polytechnic, with a registered nurse qualification. I retrained as a secondary school teacher, specialising in biology and integrated science at the University of Bristol. Until recently I have been combining researching for a PhD with part-time nursing. While studying for my PGCE I developed an interest in child health and health education in schools. I am married with two small sons and live in Worcestershire.

Tony Whittle RN, DPSN, BSc (Hons), MSc (Advanced Practice)
Senior Lecturer, University of Central England, Birmingham

I qualified as a Registered Nurse in 1983. I undertook the ENB 249 Cardio-Thoracic Nursing Course in 1984, subsequently specialising in thoracic surgical and medical nursing at East Birmingham Hospital. Periods as Staff Nurse and Charge Nurse led to the role as Speciality Manager responsible for nursing and non-nursing management of the regional thoracic surgical unit. During this time I undertook the Diploma in Professional Studies in Nursing. In 1992 I entered the Birmingham College of Nurse Education responsible for the ENB 249 Course as an Unqualified Tutor. After completing the BSc (Hons) in Education Studies (Nursing) at the University of Wolverhampton I was appointed as Nurse Tutor at the Birmingham College of Nurse Education in 1993. Since then I have specialised in the delivery of coronary care, cardio-thoracic and acute care courses. My interests lie in the role of the educator and its effects on the advancement of nursing practice. This has provided the focus for a research dissertation for an MSc in advanced practice.

Acknowledgements

Throughout this book and within others in the series we have stressed the significance of learning from experience and the central role that reflection plays in this. When we reflect on our experience of preparing *Caring Moments: The discourse of reflective practice*, we come to fully appreciate the enormous debt of thanks we owe to Hazel Alley and Sue Hampton, Policy into Practice Research Centre, University College Worcester. Their high level of computer literacy, abundance of patience, cheerfulness and commitment in trying to understand what was in our heads, will be some of our enduring memories.

We would also like to formally acknowledge our debt of thanks to all our colleagues who have contributed to this book, especially Nanette Smith, Yamini Suvarna and Karen Deeny. Writing a chapter was a 'first-time' experience for some of them. Thank you all for helping to make 'caring moments' come alive. Your stories are deeply moving and humanly significant. They are your experiences. We hear your voice.

Tony Ghaye and Sue Lillyman
January, 2000

Introduction

Caring in context

Sue Lillyman and Tony Ghaye

The overall intentions of this book are to assist healthcare professionals in their approaches to reflection and to understand how the processes and principles of reflective practices can help us make more sense of that aspect of healthcare work which we shall call a 'caring moment'. Taken together we hope that the book illustrates the important interconnections between practice and 'thinking again' about it. In other words, between action and reflection-on-action. Action and reflection need each other. They are interdependent. We hope that this book will give you ideas about how reflection can serve the purpose of helping to identify how practice can be nourished, further enhanced and improved. In some chapters the chosen moment has been reflected upon with the explicit use of a 'model' or 'approach to reflection', for example in *Chapter 5*. In other chapters (eg. *Chapter 7*) reflection is more of a kind of 'stream of consciousness'. This is the intelligent re-working and questioning of practice unaided by structured models, however flexible. Together these provide a variety of ways to learn from experience.

The book includes the word 'discourse' in its title. In Ghaye and Lillyman (2000) we explain in some detail how reflective practices should usefully be understood as a discourse. For the purposes of this book it is elaborated upon in *Chapter 1*. In short, a discourse can be understood as a set of meanings, statements, stories and so on which produce a particular version of events. There are of course many possible versions, which can be told or communicated in different forms. Here we largely use the literary form although in *Chapter 8* we stress the role of numbers in creating a 'storyline' and depicting a version of events. Also we recreate the caring moment and tell it, predominantly, from one person's perspective. However, we know that those involved in the moment may have very different stories to tell and interpretations to make. We address this in many of the chapters either by explicitly including the perspectives of the others involved (eg. *Chapter 4*) or through the empathetic understanding of someone else's condition trying to present how we have tried to make sense of their world (eg. *Chapter 3*). Throughout the book we have been mindful to safeguard the anonymity of those involved unless we have had their permission to do otherwise. Names have been used where no ethical and/or professional norms or codes have been compromised.

With the introduction of Clinical Governance through the White paper 'The New NHS: Modern and Dependable' (DoH, 1997) and quality provision in 'A First Class Service' (DoH, 1998) all healthcare professionals will be involved in identifying how they care and much more how they demonstrate quality care within their own area of practice. Caring has always been seen to be a part of the healthcare professional's role. This book provides a series of caring moments, as demonstrated by a variety of authors, within the healthcare field. It will help the reader identify how the idea of a caring moment can be thought about and lived through, and how, through reflection, using different approaches and models, quality care can be better understood, nourished and developed.

Quality care: an elusive idea?

Redfern and Norman (1990) suggest that quality care is the right of all patients and that it is the responsibility of the nurse who delivers it. It is through the chapters in this book that many of the characteristics and qualities of care are illuminated. To understand this better we have invited each author to 'frame' their thinking and contribution by focusing their attention on the selection and exploration of what we have referred to as a 'caring moment'. This has been further developed in *Chapter 2* where the connections between caring moments and critical incidents are discussed. Sadly, 'good quality' care within a healthcare setting, is often only defined by its absence. Arguably therefore, there is a need to identify what is meant by good quality care for the individual, group and organisation. This will include reference to its clinical, professional and political dimensions. The concept of quality care, according to Benner (1996), can be traced back to Socrates (469 BC) and Hypocrites in (460 BC) where the latter tried to move folk wisdom into a significant art of healing. The earliest written health records, according to Marr and Giebang (1994), were in the Babylonian Empire Circa BC 1700 where sanctions were described for providing poor quality healthcare and later through Florence Nightingale (1859) who introduced the idea of caring for the patient by putting them in the best environment for nature to act upon them. Henderson (1960) suggests that nursing care should be done for the benefit of the patient and that care is administered to assist the patient to health or a peaceful death. Care is not just related to cure. It is a much more complex idea than this. The contributions to the book illustrate this vividly.

Caring is identified by the World Health Organization (1996) as an important part of nursing practice. Among other things they note that care needs to be understood in terms of relationships, for example, with an individual, family or community. These views of care are demonstrated throughout the various chapters. Care is also associated with the notion of 'helping'. Helping includes creating a climate of healing, providing comfort, establishing a relationship and committing oneself to this relationship through that nursing care. Williams (1998) takes this further in his attempt to identify what we mean by 'quality nursing care' and suggests that it relates to the perceived degree to which patients' physical, psychological and 'extra care' needs are met. He suggests that physical needs are identified in relation to the lack of personal independence in daily physical function. Psychological needs relate to the supportive role assumed by the carer, including communication, providing information and being the patient's advocate. With regard to 'extra care needs' he suggests that this is difficult to define but is concerned with the personal touch administered during the period of care.

Astedt-Kurki and Haggman-Laitila (1992) argue that some of the attributes of care are to do with nurses' attitudes, time for discussion, individualism, listening, showing interest in, feelings and understanding the experiences of their clinical/patient. These attributes are developed further through the various chapters in the book. We should note that Phillips (1993) suggests that caring is a value-laden enterprise and that the intention of that care is often confused with achievements of the care. It is not the evaluation of care *per se*, but the means by which the individual draws on his/her knowledge, skills and attitudes to deliver that care, that identifies the values held. In other words, the caring values are evident in and through healthcare practice. Practice therefore needs to be understood as values-in-action.

Caring *vs* cure

The role of the nurse or professional allied to medicine often identifies the role of 'caring' with emotional connotations, whereas the role of medicine is often associated with a curing function. Holden (1991) asks if the medical profession does not care for, and the carers not cure? He notes the origins of the word 'care' and points out that it actually originates from the French eleventh century word for 'cure'. He therefore questions if they should be seen as two separate identities or more appropriately in a more complex, interactive and holistic relationship? The important issue here is how healthcare professionals view their role, the emphases within it and the extent to which they feel able to live out their caring values in their practice.

Conclusion

The specific role that reflection plays within the delivery of a quality care service is demonstrated throughout this book and other related books, (Ghaye and Lillyman, 2000). Reflection assists the individual in identifying and nourishing good practice. It can help us develop realistic action plans that serve to work at aspects of practice with the intention to try to enhance and improve what we do. Reflection can also serve to help us understand the difference between what we wish to do and what we are able to do as we try to care for our patients/clients. It can give us a better sense of self, self in relation to others and the organisational contexts within which our practice is embedded. This book takes the notion of a caring moment as the essence and focus of healthcare work. The contributions describe different moments and use reflective practices to explore and make more sense of each one. In this way thinking and practice are helped to move forward. Without this reflective process we are doomed to relive the experiences and mistakes of the past. We enslave and imprison ourselves rather than provide ourselves with opportunities for enlightenment and empowerment.

References

Astedt-Kurkit P, Haggman-Laitila A (1992) Good Nursing Practice as Perceived by Client: A starting point for the development of professional nursing. *J Adv Nurs* **17**: 1195–1199

Benner P (1996) *From Novice to Expert: Excellence and Power in Clinical Nursing.* Addison Wesley, Menlo Park, CA

Department of Health (1997) *The New NHS: Modern and Dependable.* HMSO, London

Department of Health (1998) *A First Class Service, Quality in the New NHS.* HMSO, London

Ghaye T, Lillyman S (2000) *Reflection: Principles and Practice for Healthcare Professionals.* Quay Books, Mark Allen Publishing Ltd, Dinton, Salisbury, Wiltshire

Henderson V (1960) *The Nature of Nursing: A Definition and Its Implications for Practice, Research and Education.* Macmillan, New York

Holden R (1991) In Defence of Cartesian Dualism and Hermeneutic Horizon. *J Adv Nurs* **16**: 1375–1381

Marr H, Giebang H (1994) *Quality Assurance in Nursing Concepts, Methods, Case Studies.* Campion Press Ltd, Edinburgh

Nightingale F (1859) *Notes on Nursing.* Harrison and Sons, London

Redfern S, Norman I (1990) Measuring the Quality of Nursing Care: A Consideration of Different approaches. *J Adv Nurs* **15**: 1260–1271

Phillips P (1993) A Deconstruction of Caring. *J Adv Nurs* **18**: 1554–1558

Williams A (1998) The Delivery of Quality Nursing Care: A grounded theory study of nurses perspective. *J Adv Nurs* **27**: 808–816

World Health Organization (1996) *Report of the WHO committee Nursing Practice: WHO Technical Report Series 860.* WHO, Geneva

1
Reflection-on-practice as a discourse

Tony Ghaye

Caring moments: Stories and experience as discourse

This is a book of stories, powerful stories. Each of the caring moments presented can be understood as a kind of story. Telling stories is a way healthcare professionals make sense of practice. Making some sense of practice when the world seems to be forever turbulent, changing and chaotic is a real achievement. Reflection-on-practice is a fundamental ingredient: reflection being a sense-making process.

> *Sense is crafted, put together with skill and care, not simply experienced as if prefabricated. We can see others, and occasionally ourselves, making sense in a way which does not seem to be conducive to productive action; it is not simply that sense is made or not made, but that there are consequences to the kind of sense that is made. Everyday sense-making is not a matter of trying to make total sense of everything. There are levels of sense with which we feel comfortable. Too much sense — too clear an understanding of everything around us — may be boring.*

(Wallemaq and Sims, 1998, p.121)

To this we might add, too little sense — being unclear about what is happening around us — is a recipe for disillusion, stress and burnout.

In the literature on reflective practice we often see a reference made to reflection as a way of turning experience into learning (Boud *et al*, 1998). But experience can also turn into stories (Driscoll, 1999a, 1999b, 2000; Bowles, 1995; Vezeau, 1993). Over time stories transform into experience. In this book the 'caring moment-as-story' is a central idea. The stories are of many sorts and told in different ways. This story-telling can be understood as a discourse in which the uniqueness of the persons involved and the situation are displayed (Harre, 1998). They are examples of what Schafer (1992) describes as, 'persons constructing and revising their various experiential selves' (p.25). Reflection is the process which fuels this reconstruction and revision for within the chapters, 'moments' are first described and then reflected upon. In essence, the caring moments might usefully be seen as the way healthcare professionals experience others, how they experience themselves and how they display or express themselves to others and vice versa. Stripped down they are about how I am to you and how you are to me.

In Ghaye and Lillyman (2000) we suggest that reflective practice might usefully be understood as a discourse. We say this because one outcome of reflection is a set of meanings, statements, stories and so on that produce a particular version of events. This is one way to understand the term discourse. Each caring moment is a particular version of events. They are a 'text' and a reflection on this. Each 'text' is some kind of socially constructed reality. However, they are also much more than this. They touch upon a number of important issues for healthcare professionals to consider. I have suggested what ten of these issues might be in this introductory chapter.

1) Single and multiple realities

They challenge us to consider the notion of multiple rather than a singular reality that we all sign up to. We do not all see and understand the world in the same way. The caring moments invite multiple 'readings' and therefore open up the possibility of appreciating alternative realities. They reflect the idea that we need to actively construct our own realities. Making sense of practice is therefore about building meanings and constructing identities for ourselves within a cultural, historical, political and clinical context. The caring moments are personal realities. They are something the writers perceive, claim to know and believe. Personal realities all differ. In healthcare we should always ask questions of the kind, 'what reality?', 'whose reality?' and 'whose reality counts?'.

2) Dominant realities and discourses

They serve to remind us that just as there are dominant realities which are often top-down or centre-periphery transferred realities there are also dominant dialogues or discourses. Some of these are very clear about what is to be understood as real and true. The discourse of technical rationalism (Schön, 1983) is still a dominant way of viewing the world for many healthcare professionals. It advertises its dominance and authority over other discourses, for example by separating theory from practice and relegating the healthcare professional to 'mere service provider' and 'technician'. For a more detailed discussion about these issues see Ghaye, Gillespie and Lillyman (2000).

3) They celebrate and prioritise subjectivity

For some in healthcare there is a distrust of all forms of subjectivity. This manifests itself in many ways. For example in the question I am repeatedly asked by students, 'Is it really ok to write in the first person?' to the obsession some have with conducting enquiries into the clinical, managerial and professional aspects of their healthcare work that always seem to have to involve very large samples, huge quantities of data, validity and reliability defined in positivistic terms and very general results. It also manifests itself in enquiries that only generate 'objective' knowledge because this seems to carry with it a sense of certainty. I do not deny the value of knowledge of this kind for certain purposes. However, we should not forget that you can indeed get large messages from small samples? We should not lose sight of the fact that everytime we make a move, a decision about what to do next, what to do with what we have gathered, what to write and what to leave out, involves subjectivities or value judgements? The caring moments here serve, in a small but significant way, to reclaim the subjective as a legitimate way of telling. They challenge the hegemony of the objective.

4) What knowledge and whose knowledge

These caring moments raise the question about what knowledge is worth knowing? Taking responsibility for one's own future development and working in a safe and accountable manner is dependent upon our ability to reflect upon our own practice and that of others. Creating and reflecting on those aspects of our work, that might be called 'caring moments', is a way of doing this. In addition to the principle modes through which the nursing profession, for example, has historically acquired knowledge, namely through tradition, authority, borrowing, trial and error, role modelling and mentorship (Ghaye *et al*, 1996) we can now legitimately add another. This is the personal, practical knowledge acquired through a reflection on the caring moments that constitute practice.

5) In whose voice?

Elsewhere we have argued (Ghaye and Lillyman, 2000) that reflective practices need to start where we are or feel we are. That in trying to enhance thinking, practice and the clinical environment we need to invite colleagues to present, perhaps rediscover and redefine their particular view of some healthcare issue they wish to reflect upon. Then they might usefully question how they currently respond to this (Freire and Faundez, 1989). This whole process requires the creation of some kind of 'text' which is the raw material that we use in the reflective process. In this book we have called these texts 'caring moments'. These moments have been 'produced' from the lived experiences of the contributors. So, the point made by Fine and Weis (1998) is highly relevant, namely, 'In whose voice do we write? Well, of course, our own' (p.27). This collection of moments enables us to hear the voices of those caring for others. It helps us understand their frames of reference, or perspectives on healthcare issues. The word 'voice' implies having something to say and a langauge to say it in. The languages used in this collection of caring moments attempt to evoke, in the reader, a sense of 'being there' too. All the 'moments' are reflected upon in different ways. In this sense they display an openness of spirit and an enquiring mind . These are surely qualities of the reflective practitioner.

6) The importance of experience

Working with experience is a central feature of reflective practice. Each caring moment is a special configuration of experience, thought about and told in a particular form. They represent the experiences of the self (and others). They are a source of knowledge and a valuable resource from which to learn. Johns and Freshwater (1998) go on to argue that they are also part of a 'transformative process'. Perhaps then we should be encouraging more healthcare professionals to tell their stories in this manner? Caring moments are about self, self in relation to others, experiences and a developmental process, all historically and culturally located and energised through reflective practices.

7) Have I told it as it really was — and does it matter?

These caring moments are retrospective accounts of healthcare, of some significance to the writers. The writers make themselves, and another, principally, the object of reflective examination. Constructing each moment has been a meaning-making process. Meaning is there, or perhaps more accurately 'in there' waiting to be re/discovered through reflection-on-action. We are of course making a big assumption here. The assumption is that these caring moments can indeed be captured and represented in a story or narrative form depicting events and life 'as it really was' (Usher, 1998). We should question any belief that these moments are indeed literal representations of what happened, was said and felt. It is perhaps better to see them as a kind of 'fabrication', a 'reconstruction and presentation (rather than a representation) of the self through the process of textual inscription' (Usher, 1998, p. 19). In other words, they are 'literary' rather than 'literal'. You may feel that at the end of the day this might not matter. If each caring moment may not be regarded as life as it really was and experienced, then I suggest we can see them as moments understood at a particular time and in a particular way and re-presented in a story form. A more pertinent question might be, 'So, what can we learn from reflecting on these stories-as-reconstructions?' Here critical forms of reflection (Day, 1999; Ghaye and Ghaye, 1998) are so important. By this I mean learning from each moment by standing back from them and asking, at least, 'how and why did that kind of incident come about?' Critical can be understood therefore 'to mean a relatively simple attitude ... in which nothing is taken as necessarily given' (Tripp, 1998, p. 37). This critical attitude towards healthcare also invites us to ask the question, 'whose interests are being served and how?' From this kind of critical reflection we might see and be able to grasp the opportunity of enhancing thinking and clinical practice.

8) The importance of workplace culture

Each caring moment is situated within an historical, cultural, political and clinical context. They should not be seen as some kind of 'free-floating incidents', coming from nowhere. Each 'moment' needs to be understood in a context. That context can be generally referred to as a workplace or organisational context. When health-care professionals work together for any length of time, for example within a unit, department, 'home', Trust and so on, they begin to come to know and to share certain values about what is right, proper, appropriate, sensitive, safe and ethical. Over time patterns of behaviour reflect these values. These values and the values-in-action constitute the 'culture' of the workplace or organisation (Thompson,

1997). Each caring moment illustrates both values held and values-in-action. But they also reflect four other important things. First, that within the notion of workplace culture is the idea of power. Power is related to our potential or ability to do something or make something happen. It is derived from the relationships and interactions between healthcare professionals who operate within the 'structures' that serve to give the organisation its identity, serve its mission and sustain it. Each 'moment' has a power dimension within them defined in this sense. Secondly, there is a political dimension to each caring moment. This is the way individuals or groups utilise power to influence values and actions. It is also about who gets what, where and how out of the 'moment'. Thirdly, each caring moment helps us to appreciate that we should think of organisations as 'social worlds' (Bate, 1994). In other words the organisation for and within which we work is a,

> *social rather than a physical entity, made up of people talking, acting, interacting and transacting with other people. Hence the idea that culture exists not so much 'inside' or 'outside' people as 'between' people.*

(p.15)

Finally, each caring moment serves to remind us that we need to think of the clinical workplace and organisation as a 'constructed' world. It is something made, something fashioned. Here I am arguing that what, among other things, is constructed are stories that speak about healthcare issues, problems, successes, heroes/heroines and villains, past, present and future actions.

9) Building worlds and selves

This collection of caring moments represents a study of discourse, in this instance healthcare discourse. It characterises discourse generally as the study of the talk and texts of social life (Stevens, 1996). Thinking about discourse in this way helps us to appreciate that through language and writing we not only 'construct' the world but also ourselves within it. Writing each caring moment has been a demanding business. It has required that the writers be conscious of how they have constructed their 'stories' and the values that have led to the particular perspective chosen. In reflecting on each caring moment they have had to be accountable for how and what they claim to know. At this point we should be mindful of the Brunerian view, namely that there is not just one 'right' way of constructing meaning and reality (Bruner, 1990, 1993). We understand and build worlds for ourselves wearing certain lenses, with certain purposes in mind and interests to serve. Caring moments are complex stories about aspects of healthcare. Perhaps we should remember that the more complex and potentially unintelligible people's lived experiences are, the greater the need for and significance of 'moments', as depicted in this book, become as ways of making experience meaningful (Boje and Dennehy, 1993).

10) Caring about others and caring for ourselves

Each caring moment is a consideration of care, expressed in different ways and occurring in different settings. They demonstrate care for others. They also reflect how certain caring values are lived out in practice and how these might be tied together into some kind of personal bundle of caring behaviours that says something important about the healthcare professional/s and the 'subject/s' involved (eg. clients, students). One of the many things we can learn from these caring moments is how expansive and multi-layered the concept of care actually is. The reconstruction of the 'moment' and the writer's reflections on it emphasise this point. Caring, as depicted in each 'moment', is clearly experiential and participatory. By this I mean grounded in relationships and actions. Safe and accountable practice and quality 'service delivery', that is governed by the ethics of caring illustrated in this book, arguably should view respectful and meaningful relationships as both means and a goal. Thus we learn from the contents of this book that caring might usefully be appreciated as being about interactions between individuals, commitment, trust, reciprocity, participation, a concern for and an acceptance of the other.

At the start of this chapter I suggested that this book might be seen as a book of powerful stories of caring. In many ways I feel that they reflect something of the essence of healthcare (Kitson, 1999) because of their focus on personhood and patient-centred care. Each moment has a history and a future. They come from somewhere and go somewhere. They are not frozen but 'dynamic texts'. In this sense they illustrate some of the fundamental components of 'caring'. Arguably these are; an intention to act, actions, justifications and consequences.

I have said before that working with experience is a central feature of reflective practices. Experience is a private thing. To make it public we have to find some means of representing it. Here, caring moments are the means. Once public, our experiences or caring moments, can be reflected upon in different ways. They can be thought about again, edited, interrogated, explored, revised and shared. Our healthcare experiences can never be displayed in their original form. They have to be represented in some way. Learning from experience, through reflection, therefore involves an important act of representation. The meaning we derive from these is constrained by the form of representation chosen. We cannot say everything in one form. Perhaps healthcare professionals need the courage to 'tell' using different forms of representation? In poetic, visual, musical, still and video forms, 3D modelling, concept-mapping, as well as narrative forms for example? I appreciate that this may well be asking some to do what they feel they cannot do. But the point I am trying to emphasise is that each representation only makes a certain amount of understanding possible. It does not tell us everything. Each one only reveals aspects of care. Perhaps what we need to be clearer about is the relevance and appropriateness of the different forms of representation in helping us move thinking and healthcare practice forward. Representing and understanding each caring moment therefore invites a level of invention and inter-pretation. I suggest that these 'moments' also invite a level of commitment. A commitment to reflect on care. Reflection is something to be reaffirmed continually in everyday practice.

References

Bate P (1994) *Strategies for Cultural Change.* Butterworth-Heinemann, Oxford

Boje D, Dennehy R (1993) *Managing in the Postmodern World: America's Revolution against Exploitation.* Kendall-Hunt, Dubuque IA

Boud D, Keogh R, Walker D (eds) (1998) *Reflection: Turning Experience into Learning.* Kogan Page, London

Bowles N (1995) Storytelling: a search for meaning within nursing practice. *Nurse Ed Today* **15**: 365–369

Bruner J (1993) The Autobiographical Process. In: Folkenflik R (ed) *The Culture of Autobiography.* Stanford University Press, Stanford, CA

Bruner J (1990) *Acts of Meaning.* Harvard University Press, Cambridge, Mass

Day C (1999) Researching Teaching through Reflective Practice. In: Loughran J (ed) *Researching Teaching: Methodologies and Practices for Understanding Pedagogy*. Falmer Press, London

Driscoll J (2000) *Practising Clinical Supervision: A Reflective Approach*. Ballière Tindall (in association with the RCN), London: chaps 6and 7

Driscoll J (1999a) Getting the most from clinical supervision: part one, the supervisee. *Ment Health Practice* **2**(6): 28–35

Driscoll J (1999b) Getting the most from clinical supervision: part two, the supervisor. *Ment Health Practice* **3**(1): 31–37

Fine M, Weis L (1998) Writing the 'wrongs' of fieldwork: Confronting our own research/writing dilemmas in urban ethnographies. In: Shacklock G, Smyth, J (eds) *Being Reflexive in Critical Educational and Social Research*. Falmer Press, London

Freire P, Faundez A (1989) *Learning to Question: A Pedagogy of Liberation*. WCC Publications, Geneva

Ghaye T et al (1996) *Theory-Practice Relationships: Reconstructing Practice, Self-supported Learning Experiences for Healthcare Professionals*. Pentaxion Press, Newcastle-upon-Tyne

Ghaye T, Ghaye K (1998) *Teaching and Learning through Critical Reflective Practice*. David Fulton Publishers, London

Ghaye T, Lillyman S (2000) *Reflection: Principles and Practice for Healthcare Professionals*. Quay Books, Mark Allen Publishing Ltd, Dinton, Salibury, Wiltshire

Ghaye T, Gillespie D, Lillyman, S (eds) (2000) *Empowerment through Reflection: The narratives of healthcare professionals*. Quay Books, Mark Allen Publishing Ltd, Dinton, Salibury, Wiltshire

Harre R (1998) *The Singular Self: An Introduction to the Psychology of Parenthood*. Sage Publications, London

Johns C, Freshwater D (eds) (1998) *Transforming Nursing through Reflective Practice*. Blackwell Science, Oxford

Kitson A (1999) The Essence of Nursing. *Nurs Standard* **13**(23): 42–46

Schafer R (1992) *Retelling a Life: narration and dialogue in psychoanalysis*. Basic Books Inc, New York

Schön D (1983) *The Reflective Practitioner*. Basic Books Inc, New York

Stevens R (ed) (1996) *Understanding the Self*. Sage Publications, London

Thompson J (1997) *Lead with Vision: Manage the Strategic Challenge*. Thompson Business Press, London

Tripp D (1998) Critical Incidents in Action Inquiry. In: Shacklock G, Smyth J (eds) *Being Reflexive in Critical Educational and Social Research*. Falmer Press, London

Usher R (1998) The Story of the Self: Education, Experience and Autobiography. In: Erben M (ed) *Biography and Education: A Reader*. Falmer Press, London

Vezeau T (1993) Storytelling: A Practitioner's Tool. *Am J Maternal Child Nurs* **18**: 193–196

Wallemaq A, Sims D (1998) The Struggle with Sense. In: Grant D, Keenoy T, Oswick C (eds) *Discourse + Organisation.* Sage Publications, London

2

Critical incidents as caring moments

Sue Lillyman

Throughout this book you will find practitioners' accounts of experiences which they have identified as caring moments. In this chapter I will identify how a critical incident, within a healthcare setting, can be used to identify some of the qualities of a caring moment and how it can assist the practitioner in developing their clinical practice.

What is a critical incident?

Critical incidents can take many forms. They provide the practitioner with an account of a personal experience through which they can identify how they develop and justify their practice. Ghaye and Lillyman (1999, p.80) describe an incident as an experience that can be:

- an incident that is an ordinary experience
- an incident where the experience did not go to plan (these may be positive as well as negative experiences)
- an incident that went well
- an incident that reflects the values and beliefs held by the individual
- an incident that identifies the contribution of qualified practitioners
- an incident that allows the identification of learning.

The incident relates to an experience which the practitioner has encountered during his/her practice. This incident is then recorded, reflected upon and analysed in order to develop, enhance or justify the practitioner's contribution to patient/client care.

There are many definitions of critical incidents, however, Tripp (1993) sums it up when he states,

> *Incidents happen, but critical incidents are produced by*
> *the way we look at a situation, it is an interpretation of the*
> *significance of the event.*
>
> (Tripp, 1993, pg.8)

For nurses and healthcare workers the words 'critical' and 'incident' both have different meanings to that described by Tripp. 'Critical', often refers to the state of condition of a patient or situation that is used in a negative or traumatic context within nursing. It also suggests an area of advanced specialist care, such as 'critical care units'. The word 'incident' also implies negative aspects of care, it is currently used in nursing when some major or significant event has occurred that may require at a later date some confirmation in a legal sense. An 'incident form' is then completed. For the purpose of this book the 'critical incident' is not identified as a negative aspect of care. I view critical incidents as experiences that have had some impact on our practice. The incident may appear trivial to other practitioners and appear unworthy of any reflection or analysis to others. The point is that every day events provide practitioners with potential learning situations and it is these that become our critical incidents.

These incidents could be referred to as an experience that had some form of emotional impact on the practitioner and sometimes referred to as 'learning experiences' to remove the negative connotations of the title critical incident. According to Love (1996), for the event to be a critical incident, it should evoke deep thought and raise a professional issue. These aspects of critical incidents are clearly demonstrated throughout this book where practitioners have encountered an experience that has affected their practice and has usually raised some emotional feelings. Rich and Parker (1995) suggest that without any structure of reflection, of an associated critical incident, analysis may potentially lead to disaffection. For this reason I advocate a structured approach to analysis as identified in Ghaye and Lillyman (1999). Critical incidents, following reflection and analysis allow the individual to identify learning from their experiences in relation to identifying new practice, the way theory interacts with clinical work and/or justifying their practice. Parker *et al* (1995) suggest that this process may be viewed as synonymous with meaningful discovery. They suggest that learning from experience always begins with reflection-on-practice and an analysis and evaluation of it. It is the latter that provides the practitioner with the evidence to move practice forward.

The value of critical incidents

For some, learning through critical incidents has been used to bridge any perceived gaps between theory and practice (Parker *et al,* 1995; Chesney, 1996). Critical incidents may also be regarded as a valuable framework for promoting reflective practice (Minghella and Benson, 1995). According to Smith and Russell (1991) they assist the practitioner in looking at a situation from multiple perspectives and heighten awareness of the complex skills within nursing. Reflecting on critical incidents is concerned with providing quality care to our patients/clients. Norman *et al* (1992) used the critical incident technique to identify perceptions of quality nursing care. This I suggest, is an aspect the individual can use for his/her own practice and in relation to clinical governance (DOH, 1997).

In the current climate of nursing practice, where practitioners are required through their *Professional Code of Conduct* (1992) and the Post Registration Education and Practice (UKCC, 1990) requirements, to demonstrate their clinical competence, critical incident analysis can play a valuable role. This process, together with the notion of clinical governance, relies on self audit by practitioners to demonstrate their levels of competency in practice. Critical incident analysis is a process that can be used by the reflective practitioner for this purpose. Saylor (1990) suggests that the ability to reflect upon one's practice is essentially for competency and therefore advocates the use of critical incidents for this purpose. Burnard (1990) argues that learning from experience, if used effectively, can have a direct and indirect effect on improving the quality of nursing education, management and care. Arguably, this is the aim not only of the individual practitioner but is also high on political and professional agendas.

Critical incidents are also identified by Schön (1983) as a valuable learning process. Smith and Russell (1991) argue that through the process of reflection-on-action an effective practitioner will be produced, able to define and redefine problems within practice. The critical incident then within this context is a valuable focus for learning.

In this book critical incidents of various kinds have been used to identify 'caring moments' within healthcare provision settings. In another book in this series, Ghaye and Lillyman (2000) which overtly links reflection with clinical supervision, practitioners have reflected upon the supervision session in order to identify and develop specific practice within a caring role. These too can be identified as 'caring moments' within practice. In Ghaye *et al* (2000) critical incidents are used in another form to identify how reflection can lead to the empowering of colleagues and clients. The incident therefore is the catalyst for reflection and the focus for helping to transform practice. Without analysis and reflection, using critical incidents becomes an exercise in describing practice and does not allow the practitioner to gain any significantly new insights or development from the event.

It is therefore the analysis that leads practitioners on to develop and enhance practice, decision-making or broaden their knowledge base. As already identified, this requires a structured and supported process to guide the individual through. We can see different approaches throughout this book where an identified model is used for reflection. For example, *Chapter 5* uses Gibbs' (1988) model as a process for structured reflection. Each stage of his cycle is identified as the individual practitioner addresses the provision of care for a patient within the endoscopy unit. This approach allows the practitioner to identify a limitation in his/her own knowledge base and a change within the unit policy relating to new staff. *Chapter 7* uses another approach to their analysis where Tripps' (1993) 'thinking strategy' is used to make more sense of a critical incident. There are many models of reflection in the healthcare literature. Each model invites the practitioner to think again about practice in a certain way. They all have the potential to enlighten. They all have limitations as well. A range of models are reviewed and critiqued in Ghaye and Lillyman (1999). In this book the range of models reviewed are finally grouped and labelled thus:

> **Structured models**
>> ie. Johns (1994)
> **Hierarchical models**
>> ie. Mezirow (1981), Van Manen (1977) and Goodman (1984)
> **Iterative models**
>> ie. Kolb (1984), Gibbs (1988), Atkins and Murphy (1994) and Boud *et al* (1985)
> **Synthetic models**
>> ie. Louden (1991)
> **Holistic models**
>> ie. Ghaye *et al* (1996)

The model used for reflection should be the choice of the practitioner. The type of incident or caring moment they are trying to come to know better and more richly may affect the choice of model.

Caring moments

Some of the caring moments described in this book relate to critical incidents that practitioners have encountered as part of their everyday work. They are often then analysed using some form of structured approach/model of reflection such as Gibbs (1988), Johns (1994) or Kolb (1984). These incidents all relate to what the authors have identified as 'caring moments'. They are incidents that have left an impression on the practitioner, such as the patient being given bad news or the group of students who demonstrated their own reflective skills with the learning environment, and provided the practitioner with an incident that they can record and reflect upon in relation to improving their own practice. Through the analysis and reflection on these caring moments practice is firmly linked to theory and issues are identified through some form of emotional response to a situation. Ultimately through reflection, care may well be improved with the practitioner being able to demonstrate their own competence within their area of expertise. Norman *et al* (1992) noted that the appropriate basic unit of analysis was not the incident itself but the happenings revealed by incidents that are critical by virtue of being important to respondents with respect to the quality of nursing care. Therefore, to stop at identifying an incident or caring moment, the descriptive phase of the process, will not be valuable to either the practitioner or the profession.

One limitation in relation to critical incidents, noted by Smith and Russell (1991) is that the retrospective evaluation of personal experience can be subject to subconscious editing. This may provide the espoused theory being identified rather than the theory-in-practice. For this reason we recommend the use of learning journals in which to record the critical incidents as they occur. This will then provide practitioners with a more accurate picture of what happened before they start to put their own interpretations on the event with the fading memory. We note that some reflection takes place within the recording of the incident, however this is the first stage of the process. The whole issue in using the critical incident analysis framework is to make the point that caring moments can be reflected upon and learned from in this way. It is one of a number of approaches to reflection that can help to move thinking and practice forward in a justified manner. Smith and Russell (1991) note that clinical knowledge develops as practical experiences are combined with the application of theoretical knowledge, with this being further redefined and extended within practice. The whole process is cyclical integrating theory and practice. Rosenal (1995) notes that the process of using critical incidents can guide the learner/practitioner through a process with which they may be unfamiliar thereby enhancing practice through experiential learning.

One view of a caring moment then can be summed up as an experience that the individual has encountered with patients, clients, colleagues and/or students that has had a significant effect on the individual and provided the basis for a learning experience on which the individual can, or perhaps should, reflect. Each caring moment throughout the book relates to either direct care or educational provision leading to improved care through a specific incident. Critical incidents are a particular way of both naming and understanding care. It is a process of moving practice forward and can be used as evidence of self-development within practice and as part of the individual's personal professional profile. Identifying these caring moments as aspects of practice that need to be thought about again is even more pertinent as nursing, midwifery and health visiting becomes more accountable through the process of clinical governance (DOH, 1997). Critical incident analysis is one of a number of approaches that can be utilised by each practitioner, in the pursuit of safe and accountable practice.

References

Atkins S, Murphy K (1994) Reflective Practice. *Nurs Standard* **8**(39): 49–56

Boud D *et al* (1885) Promoting Reflection in Learning: A model. In: Boud D, Keogh R, Walker D (eds) *Reflection: Turning Experience into Learning*. Kogan Page, New York

Burnard P (1990) Group Discussion. *Nurs Times* **86**(37): 36–37

Department of Health (1997) *The New NHS: Modern and Dependable*. HMSO, London

Ghaye T *et al* (1996) *Learning through Critical Reflective Practice: Self-supported learning experiences for health care professionals.* Pentaxion Ltd, Newcastle upon Tyne

Ghaye T, Lillyman S (1999) *Learning Journals and Critical Incidents: Reflective Practice for Health Care Professionals.* Quay Books, Mark Allen Publishing Ltd, Dinton, Salisbury, Wiltshire

Ghaye T, Gillespie D, Lillyman S (eds) (2000) *Empowerment through Reflection: The narratives of healthcare professionals.* Quay Books, Mark Allen Publishing Ltd, Dinton, Salisbury, Wiltshire

Ghaye T, Lillyman S (eds) (2000) *The Role of Reflection in Effective Clinical Supervision.* Quay Books, Mark Allen Publishing Ltd, Dinton, Salisbury, Wiltshire

Gibbs G (1988) *Learning by Doing: A Guide to Teaching and Learning Methods.* Further Education Unit Oxford Brookes University, Oxford

Goodman J (1984) Reflection in Teacher Education: A Case Study and Theoretical Analysis. *Interchange* **15**(3): 9–26

Johns C (1994) Nuances of Reflection. *J Clin Nurs* **3**: 71–75

Kolb D (1984) *Experiential Learning Experience as the Source of Learning and Development.* Prentice Hall, New Jersey

Louden W (1991) *Understanding Teaching.* Cassell, UK

Love C (1996) Critical Incidents and PREP. *Prof Nurse* **11**(9): 574–577

Mezirow J (1981) A Critical Theory of Adult Learning and Education. *Adult Ed* **32**(1): 3–24

Mingella E, Benson A (1995) Developing Reflective Practice in Mental Health Nursing through Critical Incident Analysis. *J Adv Nurs* **21**: 205–213

Norman I, Redfern S, Tomalin D, Oliver S (1992) Developing Flanagan's Critical Incident Technique to Elicit Indicators of High and Low Quality Nursing Care for Patients and their Nurses. *J Adv Nurs* **17**: 590–600

Parker D, Webb D, D'Souza B (1995) The Value of Critical Incident Analysis as an Educational Tool and its Relationship to Experiential Learning. *Nurse Ed Today* **15**: 111–116

Rich A, Parker D (1995) Reflection and Critical Incident Analysis: Ethical and moral implications of their use within nursing and midwifery education. *J Adv Nurs* **22**: 1050–1057

Rosenal L (1995) Exploring the Learner's World: Critical Incident Methodology. *J Contin Ed Nurs* **26**(3): 115–118

Saylor C (1990) Reflection and Professional Education: Art and Science and Competency. *Nurse Educator* **15**(2): 8–11

Schön D (1983) *The Reflective Practitioner.* Temple Smith, London

Smith A, Russell J (1991) Using Critical Learning Incidents in Nurse Education. *Nurse Ed Today* **11**: 284–291

Tripp D (1993) *Critical Incidents in Teaching.* Routledge, London

United Kingdom Central Council for Nursing, Midwifery and Health Visiting (1990) *Report of the Post Registration Education and Practice Project*. UKCC, London

United Kingdom Central Council for Nursing, Midwifery and Health Visiting (1992) *Professional Code of Conduct for Nurses, Midwives and Health Visitors*. UKCC, London

Van Manen D (1977) Linking ways of Knowing with ways of being Practical. *Curriculum Enquiry* **6**(3): 205–28

3

A caring moment with Peter

Ruth Hardie

Caring moments are not just experiences we live through, but ones we need to analyse and use to identify the aesthetic knowledge and experiential learning acquired. It is through these reflective practices that we give ourselves opportunities to further improve clinical practice, draw upon and use scientific knowledge appropriately, and ultimately develop and provide evidence of an 'expert' practice in action (Ghaye and Lillyman, 1999).

The caring moment

One morning, when taking the opportunity to prepare for a busy afternoon clinic by looking through the medical records of those patients booked in for pre-operative assessment; one of the staff nurses on the ward, ran into my office asking if I would go onto the ward as one of the patients was calling for me. The staff nurse appeared worried, so instantly stopping my work we hastened to the ward.

There seemed a lot of commotion on the ward, the noise level was high, and the attention was drawn to the gentleman in the corner bed who was shouting my name loudly. Knowing him well, I went instantly to his side. Peter was very agitated and distressed, clinging to my hand he exclaimed, 'I'm dying aren't I? Ruth you have always been straight with me, tell me the truth now, I'm dying aren't I?' Sitting next to Peter, and taking both of his hands into mine while looking straight into his eyes, I spoke softly to try to calm and reassure him, saying, 'I can feel your distress, and want to help you, but before we can address your fears let us try to make you feel a little calmer so that you can concentrate on what we discuss.' While continuing to speak softly, Peter was asked to breath slowly and deeply, as he was reminded of our open and honest relationship, and reassured that his questions would be answered with the same honesty.

When Peter was calmer, the curtains around his bed were closed to ensure a little more privacy. Returning to my seated position facing Peter, and holding his hands in mine whilst maintaining eye contact, he was asked what had caused his distress. He responded by saying that he had an overwhelming feeling that he was going to die imminently and that he wanted someone to tell him honestly if this was going to happen. My response was, 'Peter, what do you know about your illness?' He said, 'I know I've got cancer and that it has spread into other parts of my body.' I confirmed that this was true, and that this meant he was very ill. He then said, 'It is going to kill me isn't it?' My reply was, 'Yes Peter, the cancer will probably cause you to die, but before that, you have got a lot of living to do.' He responded, 'What do you mean?' 'You are seriously ill with advanced metastatic cancer, and you are very weak, but you have a wonderful family and you have told me that you want to spend more time with them. Having a lot of living to do, means that you should spend this stage in your life living, and doing those things which are most important for you. Talk to your family; say the things you want to say and do the things you want to do. Make every moment special, live life with the cancer, rather than die with the cancer.'

At this Peter silently cried, then squeezed my hands. He then asked me to call his wife, he wanted to see her and tell her that he loved her. Peter insisted on my staying with him while his wife came to the ward, he held my hand firmly, and whispered, 'please don't leave'. Speaking softly and calmly to Peter talking about all of the wonderful things he had told me about his wife and children, concentrating on the laughter, love, and fun they shared together, he began to smile. When his wife arrived on the ward Peter was calmer and they held onto each other both silently crying. When attempting to leave, Peter asked if I could stay for a while, he said 'I still need some of your strength.' He then turned to his wife and said, 'I feel more in control now, I know I'm going to die, but it will be when I am ready. I need to spend some more time with you and the boys first; Ruth has helped me see that. I love you, and want to tell you, I want you to remember that when I am gone.' They held each other again and, although tears, there was also a great sense of happiness. Peter soon relaxed back into his pillows exhausted with emotion, he squeezed my hand and said, 'You can go now, I thank you for your help, you have given me back my life.'

On leaving the room, my own feelings and tears surfaced, a feeling that I had done so little, but glad that it was helpful if only in a small way.

Peter died very peacefully in his wife's arms two weeks later, after saying his goodbyes to all his family and friends. At Peter's *funeral his wife hugged me, and thanked me for helping them, saying that I was in the right profession.*

My reflections on this moment

My role on the unit was that of a nurse practitioner. My job entailed seeing all elective patients prior to surgery to undertake a holistic assessment, to assess their nursing, medical, psychological, social and spiritual needs. This form of assessment helps establish trust in the nurse-patient relationship, intervening by listening and collecting information that will be useful in the planning of patient care (Allport *et al,* 1985). This in-depth assessment allowed me to get to know the patient and their families well, and ensured preparation of the inter-disciplinary team for the patient's admission. Assessment also prepared the patient for their surgery or tests, by educating them about what was involved in the procedures and what was to be expected post-operatively (Hardie, 1993). Patients benefited from this consultation as they were more willing to discuss problems with a nurse than a doctor as the problem of 'not wanting to waste the doctor's time still persists' (McLaughlin, 1978). Peter had been one of these patients. When he first came to the assessment clinic he had little understanding of his forthcoming operation, but had openly told me that he hadn't liked to ask the doctor as he felt that he was busy in clinic. That was over a year ago, and Peter and his wife had been back to my clinic many times, where we had honestly discussed his invasive cancer. He had found that some members of the inter-disciplinary team had difficulty discussing his disease and used avoidance techniques to prevent entering conversation. We had discussed that this was a form of defence mechanism to protect themselves against the pain they felt (Lichter, 1987). Peter had always commented that he wanted to be fully informed of his disease as his way of keeping control. The consultant involved with Peter's care acknowledged my communication skills and my specialist knowledge. He felt that the needs of the patients concerning communicating bad news and prognosis were met more effectively by a consultation with me rather than a doctor. This is true inter-disciplinary teamwork where there is willingness to share and, indeed, give up exclusive claims to specialised knowledge and authority (Barr, 1997). The consultant acknowledged that another professional could meet the needs of the patient more effectively.

Over that year, Peter and I had developed a therapeutic relationship based on trust, agreeing with Kaye (1996) that trust depends on reputation, competence and liking, which depend mainly on listening.

Reflection-on-practice

Reflecting on my actions helps me to make sense of what I did, did not do, might have done and what I might do when encountering moments like this again. On reflection my purpose was to ensure that Peter had been helped to maintain his quality of life. Kubler-Ross (1970) believes that all patients know the seriousness of their illness, and that what many patients and their families want is permission to be open about their worries and anxieties. Relaxation techniques were used to calm Peter sufficiently to enable us to have a conversation without causing more distress. Experience has taught me that when a person is distressed they take in very little of a conversation. Choosing my words, as our open and honest relationship seemed important to Peter, I faced him so that he could see my facial expression showing my concern. His hands were held as a caring touch demonstrates empathy, and is one way of 'giving permission' to patients and relatives to reveal their anxieties and distress (Autton, 1989). It was obvious from Peter's answer to my question, 'what do you know about your illness', that he had a firm understanding of the nature of his disease. He was feeling a sense of panic about his impending death. I personally agree with Yalom (1980), that although dying is considered a time of crisis, it can also be an opportunity for change and positive growth. It was important to me that Peter did not loose all hope and that however bad my news by confirming his fear, it was most important to offer some positive, truthful message. Hope needs an object; setting realistic goals with a patient is one way of restoring and maintaining hope (Twycross, 1997). When trying to maintain realistic goals with Peter, it seemed appropriate to concentrate on the positive aspects of his life which were achievable. With patients close to death, hope tends to focus on being, rather than achieving, and relationships with others (Twycross, 1997); in Peter's case I focused on the relationship with his family.

An important intention when working with Peter was to enable him to maintain control over his life. Working to achieve this meant acquiring an in-depth knowledge and understanding of the physical, emotional and psychological developments in the process of dying

(Russell and Sander, 1998). From my experience, and discussions with the medical team about Peter's condition, it seemed that Peter did not have long to live. What was important was that with my skills of empathy, anticipation and communication he was helped to adapt to his new circumstances (Pullen, 1995). Peter acknowledged that I had made the appropriate intervention by thanking me for giving him back his life, and ultimately he maintained control right until the end of his life, dying peaceful in his wife's arms.

Reflecting on my own professional development, the three main characteristics which have developed throughout my nursing career, and which were used to help Peter are: congruence; unconditional positive regard; and sensitive empathetic under-standing. Corey (1991) believes that congruence implies that the nurse is real, that they are genuine, integrated and authentic, without a false front. That their inner experience and outer expression of that experience match and that they can openly express feelings and attitudes that are present in the relationship with the patient. Congruence was demonstrated by my own belief that death is part of life's journey and everyone should be enabled to live life fully throughout this journey. Peter will have identified that my inner beliefs matched my spoken word. Unconditional positive regard is where the nurse communicates a deep and genuine caring for the patient as a person. The caring is unconditional, valuing and accepting the patient without placing stipulations on the acceptance (Corey, 1991). When Peter called for me, he had the confidence in our relationship to know that he would be accepted as he was; troubled, distressed, frightened and needing support, and that I would not judge him, but just try to help him. Empathetic understanding was offered by taking account of Peter's experience and feelings sensitively and accurately as they were revealed in the moment-to-moment interaction, and demonstrating my understanding of these feelings (Corey, 1991). Peter's fear facing death was palpable, his sense of loss at losing his family and his sense of losing control as the cancer weakened his body. Having empathy with these feelings enabled me to help Peter address all of these issues.

My acceptance of Peter and his condition was communicated by the quality of my presence with him, my calm approach, and my willingness to answer any of his questions, my body language and my touch. All of these attributes gave him confidence and energy, which enabled him to take control over his life. The presence of one who can talk calmly and unemotionally about death, who listens quietly and conveys understanding, goes beyond words, speaks more loudly about life and love than any words spoken, no matter how affectionately or eloquently (Autton, 1989).

The incident appeared to take a short time, in reality it lasted approximately one and a half hours. When I eventually left the room, I felt a number of emotions but, significantly, I felt a strange sense of peace. A sense that all that could be given was given and that somehow Peter's needs were met. Nursing is concerned with meeting the needs of the person and the family. For nursing to be effective, these needs have to be patient centred, which places a responsibility on the nurse to treat each patient as a unique individual (Holt, 1995).

Walton (1995) believes that working as a nurse inherently provokes anxiety as you are continually confronting issues concerning the meaning of life and the 'spirit' of people in acute distress and adversity. He feels that the nurse's challenge is to accept and work with a more aware view of oneself, and your own issues, and be able to continue to undertake the nursing, caring responsibility of working with patients as people rather than cases of clinical conditions. To cope with such underlying pressures, and to look after youself at the same time, takes strength, personal insight and energy. Walton (1995) believes that to do this you need to know who you are, what you stand for, and the values and beliefs that you hold dear. He goes on to say that, our core beliefs are our source of inner regard, strength and cohesion, and these will drive us to tackle many situations, guiding us in taking action and responding to events (Walton, 1995). Identifying my core beliefs through reflection and exploration has helped influence and change my practice. I have learnt to value myself as a significant person, with values and feelings that are important factors in giving care (Johns, 1995). Acknowledging my core beliefs when reflecting on this time with Peter has helped identify what influenced my decision-making.

How reflecting on this caring moment has helped me understand my essential caring values

Value one: *Respect*

I try to value everyone I encounter, respecting them as an individual and treating them as I wish to be treated. Peter's wishes were for honest communication and respect as the intelligent professional he was, and full information of the nature of his disease at every stage. This openness influenced Peter's reason for asking for me, knowing that I would respond to his wishes.

Value two: *Peace*

I value finding peace in my life and helping others to find peace in theirs. It was important to me to help Peter find peace in his life, to become more accepting of his condition to enable him to live life with cancer, rather than die with cancer. Helping him find some hope and to identify some realistic goals enabled him to take more control over his life, which ultimately, I believe, enabled him to find peace.

Value three: *Quality*

I value being able to deliver quality nursing care and empowering others to do the same. My role of nurse practitioner helped improve the quality of nursing care for the whole team as it enabled greater communication between the patient and the team. By undertaking a holistic assessment including the nursing, medical, psychological, social and spiritual aspects of care, I could act as the patients' advocate, helping them to address their individual needs. Holt (1995) believes that assessment is possibly the most vital stage of the nursing process as it acts as a basis for all other stages, and is essential for nurses to be able to plan good quality, individualised care.

Value four: *Time*

I value being able to provide time for others, to address individual need and time for myself. With the pressures of working and current staff shortages within a busy acute Trust, many nurses feel that they do not have enough time to deliver quality care. The role of nurse practitioner enables independent working and not being tied into the same constraints as the nursing team. Being responsible for my own working patterns gave me the flexibility to give Peter the time he needed. However, I acknowledge that this would not always be the case. For example, if Peter had called for me in the afternoon, I would have been in the middle of a busy clinic and would not have

been able to go to the ward. Having time to address patients' psychological and spiritual needs is an essential part of my work. Reflecting on this incident has caused me to identify within myself a shift of priorities, in both my private life and professional practice, and has influenced my decision-making.

Value five: *Nursing*

I value nursing as a profession and the contribution it makes to society. Nurse practitioners are viewed by some as a cheap alternative to fill the gaps left by doctor shortages (Emmerson, 1996). When setting up the role of nurse practitioner there remained a strong belief in nursing: the reasoning behind advancing my nursing practice was to improve the quality of healthcare for patients. To this end, the medical model was incorporated into my nursing practice to ensure holism, rather than adopting the medical model to the detriment of nursing (Castledine, 1996a). It is my belief that the work of nurses is to: care for patients by maintaining client dignity and self-respect; tailor care to meet individual need; educate to provide appropriate information and support; ensure competent, safe, evidence-based practice, continually evaluate practice and work collaboratively with the interdisciplinary team and act as the patient advocate (Scott, 1997). Through the advanced role, education, demonstration of my skills and collaboration with the interdisciplinary team, I was given the opportunity and empowerment to meet most of the patients' needs. In Peter's situation, there was the knowledge base, the skills and authority to discuss the nature of his disease and its progress.

Value six: *Care*

I value being able to care for patients' relatives, family, friends and myself. Caring is not exclusive to nursing, but perhaps is the only profession that has caring as its central focus (Wright, 1995). Through this meeting with Peter and his wife, there was the opportunity to demonstrate my feelings for them through empathy, congruence and unconditional positive regard. Johns (1995) believes that as nurses have become more experienced, they have tended to give away the more caring aspects of their work to junior and unqualified staff. With the advanced nursing role, caring has remained a central focus: hopefully, acting as a role model for more junior nurses will ensure caring remains one of their core beliefs. Reflection on this caring moment and discussion of the same during clinical supervision has helped me care for myself, by developing individual insight and self-awareness. This I feel has enabled me to lead a more fulfilling lifestyle (Copp, 1988).

Value seven: *Limitations*

I value being able to acknowledge my own limitations. On reflection, I would not have changed the essential nature of my actions throughout this moment with Peter. However, one aspect which was not addressed, was the needs of my nursing colleagues. It could be argued that as Peter asked for me instead of his named nurse, her role was eroded and her responsibility devalued. In this instance, Peter's named nurse was a junior staff nurse who did not have the knowledge and skills to meet Peter's needs. What should have followed this incident was a team discussion to enable all the team members to develop their expertise in this aspect of patient care. The role of the advanced nurse practitioner should include acting as a consultant and educator in all matters relating to his/her particular chosen field and role (Castledine, 1996b). When reflecting as to why this did not happen on this occasion there were a few issues to consider:

1. The incident was personally exhausting, therefore I needed time and space to recover to enable me to prepare for continued work.
2. It was an extremely busy shift for the nurses and they could not release themselves from their workload to undergo a teaching session.
3. Time was needed to reflect on the incident for personal learning.
4. When broaching the subject of discussing death with a patient, many colleagues shy away as they find it distressing to be confronted with questions they cannot or are not permitted to answer (Lichter, 1987). Therefore, the timing of such discussion is crucial in order to provide appropriate support for team members.

Thinking again

My learning from this experience enabled me to identify improvements in my practice. I have not tied myself up in knots trying to use someone else's model of reflection. Rather, I have been conscious of two things. First, the importance of knowing my professional values (Ghaye *et al*, 1996). Secondly, by trying to build a coherent and professional story there is a growing awareness within me, of the importance of the present moment, and living life with an acceptance of its foreseeable end. The awareness that death is a normal part of life helps to remove the fear surrounding it. At the same time, it enhances the importance of valuing each moment, living life to the full knowing that it will end. This awareness develops the importance of giving time to meeting patients' deepest needs, enabling them to live their life to the full within the limitation of their disease.

This reflection has changed the direction of my career in nursing as there developed in me a greater desire to help patients to fulfil their hopes, and through education, to share this knowledge with my professional colleagues. It could be argued that areas within an acute Trust hospital, need people with the ability to communicate effectively with the dying patient and relative. However, my recent move to a hospice environment is helping my ambition to fulfil the following. It is an attempt to try to summarise some of the essential attributes of patient care. It is a statement of intent and of value. It is therefore something I keep with me and try to live out in my work. I feel that,

> *A patient should be enabled to live until they die, at their own maximum potential, performing to the limit of their physical activity and mental capacity, with control and independence wherever possible. They should be recognised as the unique person they are and helped to live as part of their family (however this might be defined) and in other relationships with some awareness from those around of their own hopes and expectations and of what has deepest meaning for him.*

References

Allport *et al* (1985) as cited in Holt P (1995) Role of questioning skills in patient assessment. *Br J Nurs* **4**(19): 1145

Autton N (1989) *Touch and Exploration*. Darton, Longman and Todd, London

Barr O (1997) Interdisciplinary teamwork: Consideration of the challenges. *Br J Nurs* **5**(17): 1005–1010

Castledine G (1996a) Are British Nurses Lethargic. *Br J Nurs* **5**(1): 51–53

Castledine G (1996b) The Role and Criteria of an Advanced Nurse Practitioner. *Br J Nurs* **5**(5): 289

Copp G (1988) as cited in Butterworth T, Faugier J (eds) (1992) *Clinical Supervision and Mentorship in Nursing.* Chapman & Hall, London

Corey G (1991) *Theory and Practice of Counseling and Psychotherapy.* 4th edn. Brooks/Cole Publishing Company, Pacific Grove, California

Emmerson P (1996) Are Nurse Practitioners merely substitute doctors? *Prof Nurse* **11**(5): 326

Ghaye T *et al* (1996) *Professional Values: Being a professional, self-supported. learning experiences for healthcare professionals.* Pentaxion Press Ltd, Newcastle upon Tyne

Ghaye T, Lillyman S (1999) *Learning Journals and Critical Incidents: Reflective Practice for Healthcare Professionals.* Quay Books, Mark Allen Publishing Ltd, Dinton, Salisbury, Wiltshire

Hardie R (1993) Day Surgery Assessment Nurse. *J One-Day Surgery* **2**(3): 19–20

Holt P (1995) Role of questioning skills in patient assessment. *Br J Nurs* **4**(19): 1145

Johns C (1995) The Value of Reflective Practice for Nursing. In: Ghaye T (ed) (1996) *Reflection and Action for Health Care Professionals: A Reader.* Pentaxion Press Ltd, Newcastle upon Tyne

Kaye P (1996) *Breaking Bad News (pocket book): A ten-step approach.* EPL Publications, London

Kubler-Ross E (1970) *On death and dying.* Tavistock, London

Lichter I (1987) *Communication in Cancer Care.* Churchill Livingstone, Edinburgh

McLaughlin F (1978) as cited in Marsden J (1995) Setting up Nurse Practitioner Roles: Issues in Practice. *Br J Nurs* **4**(16): 952

Pullen F (1995) Advocacy: a specialist practitioner role. *Br J Nurs* **4**(5): 275–278

Russell P, Sander R (1998) Palliative care: Promoting the concept of a healthy death. *Br J Nurs* **7**(5): 256–261

Scott H (1997) The importance of core values in nursing. *Br J Nurs* **6**(11): 604

Twycross R (1997) *Introducing Palliative Care.* 2nd edn. Radcliffe Medical Press, Oxford and New York

Walton M (1995) *Managing Yourself On and Off the Ward.* Blackwell Science Ltd, Oxford

Wright S (1995) The role of the nurse: extended or expanded? *Nurs Standard* **10**/9(33): 27

Yalom I (1980) *Existential Psychotherapy.* Basic Books, New York

Yura H, Walsh MB (1988) as cited in Holt P (1995) Role of questioning skills in patient assessment. *Br J Nurs* **4**(19): 1145

4
A caring moment with Rachel

Val Chapman

In this chapter I intend to illuminate the notion of a caring moment by drawing on an example from the broad field of educare (those from a wide range of caring professions, including social work and school teaching). In doing so, I am trying to make the point that there is much to learn from doing this. This is a particular example, grounded in educational practice, with a focus on lived experience, reflection and learning. Although particular in kind I am going to suggest that there are a number of important and interesting principles, of a general nature, that we can glean from this that are relevant to healthcare professionals. It is a reversal in the way we might think about a caring moment. It does not look at caring moments from within healthcare but from an allied and related perspective. In this sense, it is an 'outside-looking-in' view. It is also an illustration of the principle of inter-professional learning.

The story of Rachel's cat

An observer's perspective: me looking from the 'outside in'

Rachel came into the Centre, responded quietly (eyes floored) to my 'Good morning, Rachel' and sat bolt upright at the table in front of me, her eyes fixed on her hands which were clenched tightly in her lap. In that short trip across the room her body language had shrieked of tightly controlled anguish, the absolute economy of movement signalling a taut restraint of inner turmoil.

The three boys entered next, boisterous, bantering, chorusing, 'Good morning, Mrs Taylor' in that obligatory school, sing-song style. Chair legs were knocked against tables, papers were rustled and pencils dropped as they busied themselves getting out the paraphernalia of learning.

'Morning boys.'

She rose from her seat and moved a nearby chair to sit next to the small, sad child who sat stiffly, her back rigid with tension.

'What's wrong, Rachel?' she inquired gently.

A ragged intake of breath prefaced the wobbly-voiced response, 'Nnn... nothing, Miss.'

'Rachel, look at me sweetheart... What's the matter?' she asked, searching her face for clues.

Maybe it was the endearment, or maybe it was the teacher's arm around her shoulders that cracked Rachel's resolve. Big, fat tears welled up and wetted her lashes before slipping down her cheeks leaving shiny damp trails, evidence of her misery, in their wake.

Gulping and sobbing, she finally managed to hiccup out the words, 'Oh....ohh... Miss, Benjie's d... uhh... hh... ead.' Just as she completed her statement, her older sister, Rebecca, entered the room and, hearing her sister's last words, she too dissolved into noisy tears.

The three lads looked on, concern vying with morbid speculation as to the cause of the cat's demise, while Mrs Taylor made space on her lap for two small bodies in need of a motherly cuddle.

Bit by bit, the story emerged of how poor Benjie had been found stiff on the lawn that morning. Rachel explained how they hadn't really worried when he hadn't come home the previous night since he occasionally stayed with Auntie B, an elderly neighbour who lived alone and sometimes used to borrow Benjie for company, and who 'spoiled him rotten with love.'

Gradually, the girls began to calm down as they told the group all about Benjie and his life with their family. They talked about the toys he liked to play with, sunny places he favoured for sleeping, and his bits of endearing naughtiness — the kind of snippets of life history that settle deep into a family's personal folklore and are recounted time and time again, the act of repeated sharing which exudes the glue that refreshes and strengthens a family's bonds as the years continue to pass by.

A little while later, just as the girls had reclaimed control over their voices and Mrs Taylor thought the emotional storm clouds were lifting, Rebecca suddenly wailed,

'... and then... this morning... just before we left for school... Mummy put his bowl... **in the bin!**' Huge, racking sobs ensued from both girls, their mother's pragmatic action having obviously conveyed the full impact of death's finality.

The group's planned learning activities for the morning were shelved. Instead Mrs Taylor settled the group in the comfy corner where Rachel and Rebecca were encouraged to further talk about and celebrate all the good bits of Benjie's life.

The boys (not normally known for their ability to sustain attention) listened avidly and were quick to join in with their own memories of having lost a pet, how much they, too, had cried; and one having 'even had a grandma who died once!' Led by their teacher, they talked about memories and she explained about obituaries, about how language could capture the essence of a person or a creature. Quieter now, and in control of their grief, the two girls decided they'd like to commemorate Benjie's life by writing an obituary which they could take home to share with their parents and Auntie B.

For the moment, with the distant sound of children's voices echoing from their PE lesson in the playground, peace and equilibrium were restored.

The sort of moment described above is certainly not unusual. From my perspective, the practitioner's genuine concern for her pupil (highlighted when she approached the child with a loving touch and gentle voice) was the defining 'caring moment'. The combined conscious and conscientious actions of sitting next to the child, touching and talking to her may have been instinctive, but the chosen course of action was one that was based on years of experience with and understanding of children. This caring moment captured in that snapshot of time revealed the quality of the individual both at a personal and professional level and illustrates the nature of someone who is an extended professional.

While most parents can easily relate to the instinct to cuddle a hurting child, the drive to comfort another human being in need of help reveals a more generalisable quality that may be attributed to a broader population. For some, a caring manner may originate in deeply held religious or spiritual beliefs, while for others the concern may be the overt expression of morals which have been embedded in their psyche by their experiences during their upbringing.

Such concern for the welfare of others may be a natural empathy which some possess as a result of a high 'inter-personal' intelligence[1]. Gardner advocates the view that those who are most successful in life are not necessarily those who have strengths in the logical-mathematical and linguistic areas (these being the most commonly tested intelligences in schools), but those who have high inter and intra-personal intelligence which afford sophisticated self-knowledge and an ability to understand and relate to others.

---

1. Gardner (1993) argues that there are seven kinds of intelligence: musical, bodily-kinaesthetic, spatial, intra-personal, logical-mathematical and linguistic

He illustrated his concept of inter-personal intelligence by the inclusion of a description of how Anne Sullivan managed the learning of Helen Keller who was both blind and deaf. He believed that the key to Anne's miracle breakthrough into Helen's silent, unsighted world lay in her own insight into the 'person' of Helen Keller rather than any functional knowledge of methodology or therapeutic technique.

Since he claims that sound functioning of the brain's frontal lobes play a prominent role in inter-personal abilities and recognises that a secure parenting experience and socialisation through inter-action with others are also significant factors in the development of a high inter-personal intelligence, it is interesting to consider whether or not those with such backgrounds and brain biology are almost physiologically — if not sociologically — predestined to enter the caring professions.

But how did Mrs. Taylor become the kind of person she is? What underpinned that caring moment? What experiences has she had in her own life which have brought her to this stage where she is able to operate in such an ethically sensitive and humane way? Was it reflection on her own childhood experiences? Was it a conscious reflection on her personal ethical code of practice, its origin and its validity? Had she, as a young professional, looked at her practice and asked her self questions such as, Why do I behave like this? What am I trying to do? What do I believe in? Why are these values dear to me? What should I be doing in order to feel comfortable in my practice, to know that my workplace-actions are supported by a clearly defined and firmly espoused set of values?

The carer's perspective

Well, I could see she was upset straight away — she didn't have to say anything, it was just obvious, wasn't it? She's always such a chirpy, sweet little thing, I knew it had to be something really significant.

Why did I act that way? Well… I know that we're supposed to get through the curriculum (and there's precious little time to manage that these days!), but, apart from being concerned about her (she's such a poppet) and just wanting to help her, there's absolutely no point trying to teach someone who's feeling like that, is there? They just won't take it in. No, I knew that I needed to sort it out straight away, she was obviously so upset. When you're a teacher you have to be concerned for the whole child, not just focus on the teaching aspect. And as for the lads in the class, well, I have to keep a firm hand with them 'cause they're so easily distracted. I always have to make sure they are completely occupied with activities that they're challenged by and interested in otherwise their behaviour can be quite difficult. So I suppose all those things went through my mind really... the girls being upset, the boys' behaviour, the day's tasks...

...Yes, I suppose all of that flew through my mind and I chose what I saw as the best course of action for all of them — all of us, I mean. It worked out OK, I felt that we all learned something from the experience and I think it was really important to talk about their grief and dying. It can be so scary for children when they are confronted with death like that, don't you think? Everyone was fine after play and we got a lot done later that morning.

When a professional, either wittingly or unconsciously, is the architect of a caring moment it is probable that such evident concern is the result of a cognizant adherence to a consciously espoused set of personal and professional values. Such care reflects a genuine professional commitment to living out one's values in one's workplace. It is interesting to note that despite Mrs Taylor's almost blasé acceptance of the incident as somewhat commonplace, her statement 'we all learned something from the experience', indicates that she recognised that the event was imbued with a significance for possible revisions to her future practice. This kind of care is evidence of a reflective practitioner who is dedicated to constantly striving to improve her professional practice and who views each situation as one which can be learned from. In any context, caring moments that occur may be described, either during or after the event, as critical incidents. Reflection on these has much to offer the practitioner. Although they may be snapshots of daily work by examining them, the effects of care on those involved can be seen, and interactions between colleagues can be highlighted. This also helps to make the important point that reflection-on-practice needs not to be reflection on the extra-ordinary but on the 'ordinary', the often taken-for-granted aspects of everyday practice. Reflection is not an exceptional activity brought out of the locker to try to 'solve' the problems and challenges posed by the extra-ordinary. There is much to learn from thinking again about and re-viewing the ordinary.

Though the term 'critical incident' in healthcare or police arenas of work frequently describes a life-threatening situation, Tripp (1993) and Ghaye (1997) allow a wider interpretation of the terminology. Tripp suggests that critical incidents are recognised or constructed,

> *Incidents happen, but critical incidents are produced by the way we look at a situation, it is an interpretation of the significance of the event.*

(Tripp, op cit, p.8)

... and the incidents do not necessarily have to be life threatening or dramatic,

> *It is not always the unusual or powerful events which are most critical; sometimes what is ordinary becomes extra-ordinary by its interpretation, representation or articulation.*

(Chapman, 1998, p.33)

Critical reflection and careful analysis of caring moments thus transformed into critical incidents can enhance learning and inform practice. An important feature of the transformatory nature of reflection on these incidents is the scientific and/or professional knowledge and understanding which are brought to bear in one's thinking. However, Ghaye, 1997 notes that Minghella and Benson claim that,

> ... *most incidents appear to represent inter-personal or interactional situations rather than clinical procedural problems.*

(p.80)

Tripp (*op cit*), too, recognises the affective emphasis of most incidents,

> *The high emotional charge ensures that the incidents always remain with us in spite of everything else we experience over the years. We cringe or stand tall when we touch them in memory.*

(p.98)

Caring moments are those instants in time and place which are a distillation of quality care and genuine humanity. They are critical incidents which embody professional and/or personal merit and offer much in the way of encapsulating the elements of good practice. The act of reflecting on the caring moment described in the story above transforms it into a 'lived metaphor' (Ghaye, 1997) from which much can be learned.

Critical reflection on the caring moment illustrated in this story exposes practice which correlates with Bronfenbrenner's (1979) 'ecological perspective' in the care of others. He expressed the view that children should not be perceived in isolated contexts. Every child is a 'home child' and a 'community child' as well as a 'school child'. Events, feelings and values are inextricably bound up within the complex context of the learning. Learning does not take place in isolated contexts — learning is dependent on the interaction of the individual's 'whole life' experiences. The wise professional is one who not only acknowledges the 'whole' person but who capitalises on such knowledge to bring about improvements in condition.

A participant's perspective

We was really surprised when we went into the classroom 'cos Rachel was crying and Mrs Taylor went over and asked her what's the matter. Kevin didn't hear what she said but I did, and I told him that her cat's dead. Then Rebecca came in and she started crying as well, and Miss gave them both a cuddle, but they was still crying, so then we all went and sat in the 'comfy corner'.

Mrs Taylor's always really kind and she helps you. She was talking about the cat and all the stuff he used to do, and we told her all about our pets, too, and Dave said he even had a Grandma wot died (but he always makes things up, so I don't really believe him). And then I remembered my guinea pig. He was called 'Shilling', and my mum said that was supposed to be a joke or something. Anyway, he died ages ago and I was really sad. I cried a lot when Mum found him dead in his cage, and we didn't know why he was dead or anything!

And when we was sitting in the comfy corner I remembered him, and it made me feel kind of funny, and then I felt sorry for Rebecca and Rachel 'cos their cat had died.

A caring moment may appear very differently to each of those who were present when it occurred. Reality is an interpretation of the world from an individual's perspective. Thus, when examining the same caring moment from the different viewpoints of an observer, an insider, and a participant observer, the interpretation of the event and certainly the emphases will not necessarily be the same. In relation to the incident recounted, in the practitioner's mind this was not an exceptional event but nonetheless one which needed sensitive management and, in the short term, was appreciated as significant for further reflection.

In the participant observer's view, (my view) the defined caring moment was wholly un-noteworthy since this kind of caring behaviour was what the children had learned to expect from their teacher. For Wayne, though, the whole incident determined a significant point in his inter-personal development marked by his realisation that he was truly able to relate to how another child was feeling.

A caring moment is not an accident of good fortune; it is action underpinned by the practitioner's sound knowledge, skills and understanding of their chosen field. Within any professional context, the basic human needs of the client group (such as sufficient heat, light, and physical comfort) are, of course, vitally important (Maslow, 1970), and a basic level of professional competencies which includes a positive commitment and an ability to relate to and to motivate others are also of fundamental importance. All of these competencies must harmonise with the institutional policies, custom and practice. Caring moments are those incidents that tie policy, practice, the organisation and the individual together in that they are underpinned by competence and theory but are also supplemented by sound personal values and principles.

In discussing her management of the incident, I identified a tension in her professional duties. At one level she felt legally obliged to her job (to deliver the curriculum), after all, she was paid to carry out her duties as identified in her contract; but, at a deeper level, she was experienced enough to realise that the identified primary duties were superseded by her wider professional commitment to the well-being of her charges — she acted as she did, not just out of common human decency, but from a professional understanding of the needs of those in her care.

That said, she needed to feel confident and justified in her choices since she remained answerable to her employers. It was imperative that she would be able to offer a valid defence of her professional decision, if necessary, in order to justify her practice (for example, to an inspection by anyone in authority).

She demonstrated a proficient knowledge and understanding of her professional context and, in her sensitive management of the situation, achieved a successful and beneficial outcome for all concerned. She acted in accordance with the holistic needs of those in her care. This 'emotional intelligence' (Goleman, 1995) is a hallmark of effectiveness for those in the caring professions.

In dealing with the incident in a caring and emotionally sensitive way, she also displayed the quality of flexibility. She was sufficiently confident and knowledgeable in her practice to digress appropriately to the needs of those in her care. As professionals gain experience and expertise, they develop more choices in their practice, but this extended tool kit means that they also need to develop sophisticated skills in choosing appropriately. Though skilled and intelligent practice can become automatic (judicious choices being made at almost an instinctive level), it is necessary to guard against complacency which frequency and/or habit can precipitate.

It has been suggested that professionals should aim to move through a learning process, progressing from unconscious in-competence, through conscious incompetence and conscious competence, to unconscious competence. However, it may be argued that action researchers, in healthcare and allied professions might believe that the state of unconscious competence is a somewhat smug and static condition. To be an effective action researcher requires dedicated critical reflection on practice — continual and systematic review of negated values which leads to action for improvements to practice.

The originator of the caring moment told here showed keen powers of observation and a detailed knowledge of those in her care. She was able to prioritise needs and draw on her substantial professional experience and expertise in order to manage the situation successfully.

This practitioner also recognised the importance of individual perceptions. She understood that what might appear a somewhat trivial occurrence was, to Rachel and Rebecca, a traumatic and life-changing episode. Everyone has a different life map, his/her own individual version of reality. Reality may be regarded as multi-faceted, multi-layered and existing differentially for each individual. Such sensitivity to the perceptions of others is another feature of emotional intelligence, the ability to see things from another's perspective fosters positive relationships.

For men and women are not only themselves; they are the region in which they were born, the city, apartment or farm in which they learned to walk, the old wives tales they overheard, the food they ate, the schools they attended, the sports they followed, the poems they read, and the God they believed in.

(Somerset Maugham, 1945)

When critical incidents such as these 'caring moments' are shared with colleagues, the professional dialogue that ensues can be transformative for all concerned. Practice may be evaluated against criteria which indicate good clinical/professional care. When an individual practitioner examines a phenomenon, it is like a single beam of light shining on an object from one direction, illuminating just one aspect of the phenomenon; but a group of practitioners focusing their collective professional body of knowledge and different experiences on a phenomenon is akin to focusing a number of intense, powerful beams of light on an object from a variety of directions. In this way, the object is illuminated from all angles, and a more informed view and a better understanding can result.

So it may be seen that professional discourse on caring moments can highlight good practice and questions should be asked of the kind,

- 'What have I learned from that experience?'
- 'What, in that situation, was well managed? In what way?'
- 'How might that situation have been better managed?'
- 'How far did I live my values out in my professional practice here?'
- 'How did others in the situation feel?'
- 'What implications are there for future practice for me? For others?'
- 'Was I able to meet the demands of my job?'
- 'Was there a conflict between the demands of the job and my personal value system?'

These questions fit within the spiralling cycle of professional practice identified by Ghaye *et al* (1997, p.34). Answers to questions such as these allow the reconstruction of theory-practice relationships that inform future improvement. Examining one's responses in the workplace in relation to others allows both subjective and objective evaluation of practice. In making claims for improvement, one can utilise the analysis as evidence of one's increasing competence, not just in professional practice, but in one's level of reflective practice too.

From this professional dialogue between peers it then becomes possible, at the highest levels, to synthesise individual and collective improvements with systemic and cultural improvements in the organisation; to identify and evaluate links between enhanced professionalism and empowered carers; and to generalise from specific examples to the more global issues for care.

In summary, consideration of caring moments has much to offer the practitioner both on an individual level and as part of a team. In reflecting on the elements of good practice exemplified in a caring moment, generic competencies can be identified which may inform the practice of others.

In Mrs Taylor's case these competencies included a detailed knowledge of her chosen field, a sound theoretical knowledge base, wisdom, keen powers of observation, skill, commitment, an ability to motivate others, and sensitive understanding of those for whom she had responsibility. She also demonstrated a clear understanding of the essential consideration of individual differences, not just in terms of individual needs but also in terms of sensitivity to people's individual perceptions; she exhibited confidence in her choice of action, exercised emotional intelligence in her decision-making, and demonstrated dedication to her espoused values and principles.

In reflecting on her own caring moment (in this case captured by me, a participant observer), Mrs Taylor will continue to find ways to improve her practice; sharing the event and the process of reflection with others will enhance their professional practice too. Sharing and discussing caring moments increases our ability to identify and learn from other such incidents. We are enabled to recognise these events which embody good practice and compassion. Our ability to discern such incidents is enhanced so that these caring moments — shining examples of humanity — appear as if randomly scattered throughout our working life, and, like finding the rainbows made by oil in puddles, we can continue to be surprised and delighted at finding goodness where we sometimes least expect it.

References

Bronfenbrenner U (1979) *The Ecology of Human Development.* Harvard University Press, Cambridge, MA

Chapman V (1998) *Moving Experiences: The Integration of a Neuropsychological Approach with Parental Perceptions in Developing an Understanding of Developmental Co-ordination Disorder.* Unpublished Doctoral Dissertation, University of Coventry

Ghaye A (1997) Some Reflections On The Nature Of Educational Action Research. *School Libraries World-wide* **3**(2): 1–10
Goleman D (1995) *Emotional Intelligence — Why It Can Matter More Than I.Q.* Bloomsbury Publishing Plc, London
Maslow AH (1970) *Motivation and Personality*. Harper & Row, London
Maugham S (1945) *The Razor's Edge*. Reprint Society, London
Tripp D (1993) *Critical Incidents in Teaching*. Routledge, London

5

A caring moment with Ann

Sarah Mann and Tony Ghaye

According to Burnard (1991) all practitioners need to improve practice and find better ways to care for patients. Through this chapter I will draw upon a 'caring moment', which I will also call an 'incident', that occurred early in my nursing career and use Gibbs' (1988) reflective cycle to demonstrate how practice can be interrogated and learned from through systematic and repeated reflections.

I work in an endoscopy unit which forms part of a larger day surgery unit. There are a variety of investigations carried out within the unit including, gastroscopies, sigmoidoscopies, colonoscopies and bronchoscopies. In recent years improvements in technology have meant that the investigations are relatively quick and painless, although they remain uncomfortable, for the patient. Due to these improvements in procedures and the fast turnover of patients, the skills required by the nurses within this unit differ from their peers on wards or within the community setting. These skills specifically relate to the reduced period of time allowed for building a rapport or relationship with the patient. Skills of assessment are also important to the nurse within this area, as patients' physical, psychological and emotional needs must be assessed in a short period in order to deliver a high quality of nursing care. The nurse must also be competent in the admission of patients, recovering patients from the sedation following the investigation and discharging the patient home or back to the ward. It is relevant to note that the majority of patients are informed of the investigation results prior to leaving the unit, this may involve giving the patient a serious diagnosis.

Using Gibbs' (1988) model of reflection I have been able to reflect on and analyse the following incident in a positive manner. This model is often drawn as a cycle and is shown overleaf.

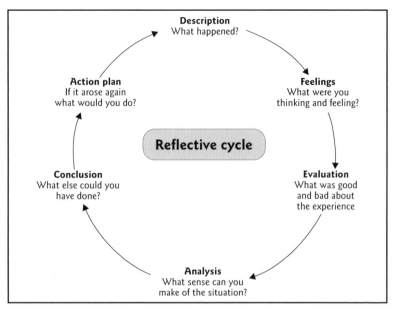

Figure 5.1: Model of Reflection (Gibbs, 1988)

Describing the incident

Gibbs notes that the first part of the reflective cycle is to describe the incident or caring moment. Such a moment occurred during my first week in this post in the endoscopy unit at this hospital and has remained with me for the past two years.

Ann was like most patients attending the endoscopy unit. It was her first visit and she was accompanied by her husband. She appeared apprehensive, however she attempted to hide her fears. Her assessment revealed a history of bowel problems. I was able to explain to her what she could expect to feel, although she would be sedated through the procedure, and that she would be given some idea of her diagnosis before she left the department. A rapport was soon established and Ann talked about her planned visit to see her daughter in America and the plans she had for her early retirement from work. Ann's colonoscopy was abandoned part way into the procedure due to her discomfort. She had, however, no recollection of this following the procedure as she was sedated. I was then to care for her during her recovery period. A barium enema followed the procedure to confirm a diagnosis. This was not planned so the procedure was explained to Ann and reasons given.

Following the barium enema I accompanied Ann and her husband while they talked to the consultant about the diagnosis. Ann was informed by the consultant that a carcinoma of the caecum had been identified and that she would require surgery the following week. This would result in a permanent colostomy.

Describing my feelings

Reflecting on it has allowed me to analyse my feelings and my concern about my own lack of skills at the time, ie. of letting the patient down, of being in too much of a hurry to get on with the next task, of not knowing what to say and therefore avoiding saying too much. Nurses' training does not cover in great detail the communication needed when dealing with seriously ill patients (Walsh and Ford, 1990) and, as a newly qualified practitioner, I felt inadequate to do this competently and confidently.

As expected, when being informed of such news, Ann's reaction was one of shock. In the space of one morning her plans had been turned around and her world had collapsed. The consultant explained that although the diagnosis was bad, the prognosis was good as they had discovered the growth in its early stages. It was at this stage that Ann wanted to know what to do next. I did not know. I did not know who to contact to seek advice for her or how the hospital procedures worked. An appointment was made for a visit in three days to see the consultant, allowing her time to reflect on the information she had received. My inadequacies, I felt, were that I had not done anything for this patient. She had left the department and I continued with the next patient. Reflecting on this incident two years later, I still feel inadequate and guilty as I was not able to help in a constructive manner or offer comfort to Ann at the time in the way that I felt I should.

Evaluating

Ann was instantly likeable. She was easy to talk to and forthcoming with information. I felt the preparation for the procedure had been completed and the care was of an appropriate standard. It was the telling of the information to Ann that had the most bearing on my feelings. I was also shocked at the results. I was upset for Ann and her family and felt my own inadequacies in offering practical advice or help in this situation. I was angry with the consultant for not telling me the diagnosis before consulting with the patient and allowing me to come to terms with the news for myself before assisting the patient. I was also angry with myself for not asking him what the diagnosis was. Such anger and wanting to direct it at someone is a natural reaction. The consultant's main concern was for Ann in wanting to tell her the diagnosis as soon as possible. On reflection, I am not sure if he felt I was there to support him or Ann. I now feel that communication could have been better between ourselves as members of a multi-disciplinary team in the provision of care.

In trying to evaluate or to make sense of this 'moment' I think that few good things came out of this experience. From Ann's point of view she did have an early diagnosis but, what of her psychological and emotional care? From the departmental point of view it could be deemed a success. The patient attended, was treated, diagnosis made and curative surgery planned. This perception leaves me feeling cold: questioning whether we did care for the patient in an holistic manner. Are we seeing patients as whole, or just as 'the colonoscopy in cubical four'? I felt that while Ann's physical needs had been met, her psychological and emotional needs were neglected.

Analysing the incident

In order to ensure that these other needs are met, time should be taken with the patient. It is quick and easy to give someone the facts but treating them as a whole person takes longer. There are a great many issues relating to this incident. My values of nursing were being challenged. I needed to support this patient while coming to terms with the information myself. My ethical knowledge (Carper, 1978), which deals with the moral code that we hold as individuals, was being compromised. I knew we needed time and that my silence in the circumstances was due to my own inadequacies. The scientific knowledge that should have been taught within the theoretical part of my training did not correspond with the practice that I was now experiencing. My beliefs in patient care were also not being played out in relation to the support that I could have found for this person as I was unaware of the facilities within the hospital at this time.

Conclusion and action plan

Reflection, according to Jay (1995), heightens self-awareness and enables the individual to gain an increased understanding of the effects that past experiences have on care delivery. This is certainly true as I reflect on this incident. Several issues concerning my own theory/practice knowledge gap and the care of future patients were identified. Gaps in personal knowledge were also identified by this incident. For example, I later found out that the hospital has a stoma nurse and contact names could have been given. This highlights the issue of new staff and how they are inducted within the unit and hospital. There is a need to give new staff a broader organisational picture so that they can use this information with their patients if necessary.

Using the Gibbs model helps me to think beyond my initial feelings and identify; the strengths and limitations of my own knowledge, procedures that could be improved, and the holistic manner which we, as healthcare professionals, need to address the patient. As I reflected on my practice in this kind of systematic manner I have learned that the finding out of information and the communication skills required when informing patients of bad news, are areas that I have to address. The reflective process has given me the clarity of thinking and incentive to do something about this. I now feel in a position to assist others. The action plan following this reflection includes the gaining of new skills, changing of unit policy in relation to the induction of staff and the improvement of patient care in relation to their psychological and emotional needs.

Reflecting on my reflections some time later

In continuing to think about this caring moment with Ann some time later, I feel that there is much more that I have learned. What follows is therefore my attempt at a kind of meta-reflection. That is to say, I want to enter the final part of this chapter by 'thinking again' (Clandinin and Connelly, 1995) about what I learned, or think I have learned! I wish to claim that I have learned that there are many ways to reflect on my practice. At the time I opted to use a reflective process that is most appropriately described as a 'cycle'. This seemed comfortable and natural. It resonated nicely with 'where I was at' in my own professional development at that time. Ghaye and Lillyman (1999) point out that cycles have an unfinished business feel to them. They argue that out of the stopping point called 'action plan' come new clinical and managerial actions, encounters and situations. These can be understood more deeply and richly by asking again the first of Gibbs' questions namely, 'what happened?'.

I think I really began this learning cycle in the way suggested by Atkins and Murphy (1994). That is to say, with an awareness of uncomfortable feelings and thoughts. I now appreciate that this is only one of many starting points. We often begin with the things that went less well or the things that we feel inadequate about in some way. Reflection-on-practice is not just an exercise in remedial action. It is not just about putting something 'right', even if this is known and possible in some way. I still feel that reflective cycles or spirals are useful to busy practitioners. They can help the individual. They are relatively uncomplicated to understand and therefore not too off-putting. Perhaps the most important thing is that they convey a clear message that learning is a lifelong business. It is a continuous developing process dependent upon active reflection and reflective action (Ghaye and Lillyman, 2000). But I have also learned that no one 'model' can do it all. Each has limitations. The one I used and present here does not really help me to reveal the importance of my nursing values in trying to make sense of practice. It does not lead me into thinking about the powerful organisational culture that serves to help or stifle my practice. These frameworks are useful if used wisely. We should avoid becoming enslaved by them. Structured reflection makes good sense but can be enriched if done collaboratively, more publically and, for example, with adequate support.

Ghaye and Ghaye (1998) suggest that irrespective of any kind of model of reflection, improving practice through reflection requires us to:

1. Problematise what we do:
In essence this is about reflecting on what is happening and why and linking this to what our intentions are and why we hold them.

2. Create a 'text': This means we have to reflect on something. A 'text' or record of what has happened is the starting point. The text is the evidential base, derived from practice, that is our raw material to work upon.

3. Confront ourself/ ourselves: They suggest that questioning practice is the key process here. The challenging thing is to come up with answers to what questions, asked by whom, when?

4. Refocus and be creative: The big issue here is that reflection needs to have a consequence. Through questioning what we do, with confidence and support, we give ourselves a chance to open up new possibilities and new directions for improved healthcare action.

In more general terms my reflections on this 'caring moment' with Ann has led me to understand that reflecting on practice is more than just reflecting in some speculative way. It implies a commitment to at least try to improve what I/we think and do in the unit, our local policies and, if possible and appropriate, improve the 'system' within which practice is embedded and policy is generated. For most practitioners trying to tackle the system might be envisaged, but it might be a massive step to try to follow this through. A duty of care and a commitment to continuously improve client care is a moral commitment. Together these things begin to say something about the nature of being a reflective practitioner. Eraut (1993) is helpful in this respect as his work enables me to appreciate that this can be seen in relation to:

- a moral commitment to try to serve the interests of my clients/patients by reflecting on their well-being and their progress and by making decisions about how care can most appropriately be enhanced
- a professional obligation to review the nature of my clinical work and the effectiveness of what I do (as well as others) in order to continuously try to improve the quality of care
- a professional obligation to continue to develop my practical nursing knowledge both by personal reflection on practice and through my interactions with others.

This caring moment with Ann has served as a catalyst for other kinds of learning. For example, it has taught me that reflection is indeed a process of turning experience into learning,

> *It is not idle meanderings or day-dreaming, but purposive activity directed towards a goal.*

(Boud et al, 1998: p.11)

Apart from the important goal of striving to improve practice, there are other goals. For me, at this point in time, another one is to use reflection to help me to maintain safe and accountable practice in a rapidly transforming healthcare service (DoH, 1998). To complicate things further our society is also rapidly changing. One consequence of this is that we are faced with an increasing chaos of choice, social and professional identity. Some features of this age are instability, complexity, transience and lack of conformity. Given this general scenario, healthcare professionals need support and guidance in trying to make sense of and survive these unstable and unpredictable clinical contexts. The healthcare professional in the twenty-first century will need to be flexible, responsive and creative at work. I have learnt that the core to being creative is a willingness to reflect critically on practice and to adapt plans and practice accordingly (Craft, 1997).

One last point. In reflecting again on my caring moment with Ann, I have come to understand more clearly how 'reflection-on-practice' is not simply about 'learning from experience' in some neat, tidy, safe and cosy manner. The two phrases are not synonymous. There is a difference that makes a difference. To learn from experience we need to give experience meaning in some way. Understanding does not come from my experience alone. Understanding experience and having an opportunity to learn from it requires, for me anyway, some set of principles and processes that help to make sense of practice. This is the role of reflection. Reflection is not just linked to a notion of learning that is cumulative and incremental. In other words, as we get more experienced in practice we get more ideas, more knowledge and more skills. This is joining reflection with an idea of learning as a quantity. This is a very limiting and skewed view of reflection. Reflection is fundamentally about a conception of learning that is to do with the quality of our perceptions and how we see things. Achieving this can be uncomfortable and feel from time to time anything but cumulative and incremental. The reflective process often requires us to 'unlearn'. This does not mean to forget. It means to unravel the complex whole of clinical practice and try to knit it all up again. It is in this process of reconstruction that we might see further, deeper and more clearly and, in doing so, come to know what is indeed a caring moment.

References

Atkins S, Murphy K (1994) Reflective Practice. *Nurs Standard* **8**(39): 49–56

Boud D, Keogh R,Walker D (eds) (1998) *Reflection: Turning Experience into Learning*. Kogan Page, London

Burnard P (1991) Improving through Reflection. *J District Nursing*, May: 10–12

Carper B (1978) Fundamental patterns of knowing in Nursing. *Adv Nurs Science* **1**(1): 13–23

Clandinin J, Connelly M (1995) *Teacher's Professional Knowledge Landscapes*. Teacher's College Press, New York

Craft A (1997) Identity and Creativity: educating teachers for postmodernism? *Teacher Development* **1**(1): 83–96

Department of Health (1998) *A First Class Service: Quality in the New NHS*. HMSO, London

Eraut M (1993) *Developing Professional Knowledge within a Client-centred Orientation*. Unpublished paper, University of Sussex

Ghaye T, Ghaye K (1998) *Teaching and Learning through Critical Reflective Practice*. David Fulton Publishers, London

Ghaye T, Lillyman S (1999) *Learning Journals and Critical Incidents: Reflective Practice for Healthcare Professionals*. Quay Books, Mark Allen Publishing Ltd, Dinton, Salisbury, Wiltshire

Ghaye T, Lillyman S (2000) *Reflection: Principles and Practice for Healthcare Professionals*. Quay Books, Mark Allen Publishing Ltd, Dinton, Salisbury, Wiltshire

Gibbs G (1988) *Learning by doing: A guide to teaching and learning methods*. Further Education Unit, Oxford Brookes University, Oxford

Jay T (1995) The Use of Reflection to Enhance Practice. *Prof Nurse* **10**(9): 593–596

Walsh M, Ford P (1990) *Nursing Rituals: Research and Rational Actions*. Heinemann Nursing, Oxford

6

A caring moment with students

Sue Lillyman and Tony Whittle

In the introductory chapter of this book the notion of 'caring' for the healthcare worker was addressed. Here a different perspective is taken where a 'caring moment' is identified with a group of students within an educational setting. A critical incident is used to explore the experience, as described in *Chapter 2*. This incident is analysed to demonstrate how reflecting on a caring moment, can help to identify how education contributes to nursing care (Ghaye and Lillyman, 1999). To do this we shall draw upon Tripps' (1993) critical incident analysis. The critical incident discussed in this chapter occurred within an educational institution and relates to one group of students undertaking a BSc (hons) in clinical nursing studies programme.

The critical incident

The authors are part of a team that teach on a part time, post-registration degree programme for registered nurses who are studying to gain a university awarded degree and a specialist practitioner qualification awarded by the English National Board, as described by the United Kingdom Central Council (UKCC, 1990). The course curriculum has an underlying philosophy of reflection-on-practice and contains a compulsory module on reflective practice which, in this instance, relates to clinical supervision within the first semester. This reflective practice module assists the students in identifying and gaining reflective skills and sensitivities that are continually developed throughout the two-year programme and hopefully throughout their nursing career (Reed and Procter, 1993).

The cohort of students to which this chapter refers were commencing their second year/third semester of the programme and attending an optional clinical module relating to their specialist area of practice. At this stage the students had completed three compulsory modules (including the one on reflective practice/ clinical supervision) and at least one clinical module.

The incident focuses upon one particular session within a specialist module delivered as part of the BSc clinical nursing studies degree. It was planned by the lecturer that the session was to be an initial examination of the student's role as a specialist practitioner in relation to the modules' particular speciality. Questions were formulated to enhance reflection by the students on their role within the modules' related area of practice.

This particular session was in the afternoon and followed a morning session which had examined the student's values in relation to wider issues of healthcare. The 'actual' session quickly diverted away from the 'planned'. The student's thoughts had been stirred by the contents of the morning session and initially the lecturer had to almost 'debrief' the students. This, however, did not inhibit the flow of the session towards the planned discussion and seemed to enhance the student's reflection upon their role in the specific area of practice. What became apparent during the session was the student's ability to identify relevant research, understand the notion of evidenced-based practice, ethical and legal issues, sociological and psychological aspects that related to patient care and reflect on their own experiences from clinical practice.

The discussion flowed freely and required minimal prompting from the lecturer. At the end of the session the students evaluated informally what they had gained. The students identified how they were able to use reflective skills, apply learnt knowledge and contribute confidently to the session. They identified how they had moved their knowledge base on further within the session through peer support. The main issue for the authors was not however specific to the clinical content of the session. It was more about how the students had realised what they had learnt within the course as a whole and how they had been able, through reflection, to verbalise this and demonstrate a higher level of thinking in relation to their own specialist field of practice.

Analysing the incident

To analyse this incident Tripps' (1993) 'thinking strategy' is utilised in order to identify the student's development. This is analysed through the student's ability to use critical thinking relating to clinical practice. The contribution of educational input is reviewed in relation to developing a reflective practitioner and a sound knowledge base in clinical practice. This strategy, according to Tripp, guides the authors' reflections on what has happened within the group and how this incident related to the educational theory and philosophy underpinning the BSc (hons) programme. Tripp (1993) suggests the use of a particular thinking strategy as a process that helps to frame a deeper reading into the given event.

Plus, minus and interesting

Here Tripp bases his analysis on the work of de Bono's (1987) 'CoRT Thinking' programme. Primarily, a review of the good (plus), minus (less good) and interesting ideas are identified within the situation. He suggests this process helps to provide general principles and assists in the evaluation of the incident.

Plus

The good points identified by the authors for this incident include:

- good group interaction with each other and the willingness to share
- increased learning identified by the students relating to previous learning
- feeling of worth for the students in relation to their specialist area of practice
- valuing each other's practice and knowledge within a peer group setting.

Many of these points identified also related to the lecturer; feelings of doing things right and seeing a method of facilitation in progress confirmed beliefs held by the lecturer in terms of his/her educational philosophy. From the students' perception the incident demonstrated how they had developed throughout the programme, and the level to which they could debate and relate relevant scientific and experiential knowledge and research to the subject under discussion. The demonstration of 'knowing how' and 'knowing why' was evident within their discussions as they related their underpinning knowledge base to clinical practice. One of the main aims in nurse education is to produce a competent practitioner; the ability to problem solve and apply past experiences to new situations is vital in producing an expert nurse (Condells and Elliot, 1989). This relates to the area of the competent practitioner and the ability to define what constitutes competence at different levels of practice (Lillyman, 1999). The lecturer noted that this process of education had benefited the students in relation to their development and ability to critically analyse; skills that would be taken back and applied to the clinical environment. This can be identified as working a higher level of practice to those individuals who are noted by Benner (1984) as being novice or competent at the point of registration. These advanced skills provide the student with the ability to return into their area of practice and make a direct contribution to the improvement of patient care. For the student, the good part was their realisation that they did know and understand what was being taught through the programme and why they were performing skills relating new knowledge to theory, and generating new knowledge, thereby reducing the theory practice gap. The students felt that they were confident and able to contribute with their peers in discussion and that their individual contribution was valued by all within the group.

A further plus point was that the students had demonstrated how they integrate knowledge drawn from other modules into their critical thinking.The degree is based upon a modular scheme which Pendleton (1991) argues differentiates and compartmentalises knowledge. This compartmentalisation is subject to and influenced by subject boundaries (Bernstein, 1977). In this example, the students were able to cross these boundaries and demonstrate linkage of subjects and bring different facets to their thinking in relation to clinical practice.

Minus

- letting go of the session and chance-taking by the lecturer
- potentially failing to achieve identified learning outcomes of the session
- not valuing each other's contribution and listening to each other
- group failing to contribute if feeling threatened or dominated by one or more individuals within the group
- leaving the subject at a tangent, with discussion becoming unrelated to the subject
- failing to be fully aware of where the discussions were leading and lacking confidence in the subject to move in any direction
- not accepting student differences or valuing own knowledge base for the lecturer.

For the lecturers this could potentially have been a negative part of the programme as they let go of the subject and allowed the students to explore their own knowledge base. This process and approach to learning and teaching required the lecturer to be confident in relation to their own knowledge base and secure in knowing that they themselves were advanced practitioners within this area (Whittle, 1999). Gagne (1985) states that the discussion class is not primarily concerned with learning at all, but with the transfer (generalising) of what has already been learned. Laycock and Munro (1966) claim that transfer is not automatic and must be taught. This would then need addressing within the sessions. It must be questioned as to whether the students were learning from their own discussion, or through relating the taught theory into their own clinical practice through reflection. The authors would suggest that the latter is the case. These students were learning and applying the theory into their practice through reflection, as the students were learning through discussion and transferring skills had been learnt along their programme/career. Rogers (1989) notes that learning is partly to do with practice and partly with self-confidence. Here we can identify how far the students' confidence had developed in their ability to articulate their knowledge base to each other and the lecturer who was facilitating the session. For the students this could have become an embarrassing time if the group had not been prepared to take the lesson forward through participation and the sharing of information. If no one had entered into the conversation then the session would not have identified how they had developed as individuals in relation to their own learning or if individuals had dominated the discussion. Therefore, for this incident the minus was mainly the potential for things not to work. From the curriculum view it may relate to the learning outcomes of the session if it was identified that these had not been met within the session.

Interesting

- teaching philosophy.

The session was interesting in relation to the approach to learning that had been identified by the students. Most students, according to Rogers (1989), are strongly motivated by their desire to gain skills and knowledge that they can use immediately and in practical ways, this is evident with the post-registration student who has often chosen to commence a course. The approach to adult learning can be identified throughout this curriculum.

Alternatives, possibilities and choices

This aspect of the analysis asks us to look at alternative ways of viewing the incident, identifying things that might have happened in the situation described if it had not gone as planned. This approach to analysis is not normally performed when an incident is perceived to have gone well. Tripp notes that human nature does not usually question good incidents. However Tripp notes that this process assists the analysis for future incidents and could identify potential problems as identified in the minus section or how the experience could be built upon for future groups. For this incident there could have been a very different outcome if the students did not feel safe and confident to contribute to the session. The lecturer may have found him/herself in a situation where it was necessary to take over and lead a session on the subject in hand in a more pedagogical approach. Another outcome of this process could have been to be more creative on the part of the lecturer and not to have had the timetable filled in at all, but to have given the module to the students empowering them to choose the topics that they wished to explore within their module. The lecturer then becomes the facilitator of the subject rather than the deliverer and a true approach to open learning is achieved, as identified by (Knowles, 1975).

Other points of view

For this session it was useful and, indeed, relevant to seek the students' perception of the session and how they felt it had been delivered. To only take the perception of the lecturer may have not been a true account. The lecturer may have felt 'good' for a variety of reasons and had a group that felt vulnerable, undervalued, with dwindling confidence in the lecturer if they were expecting a different approach to the lesson. Here the session was evaluated and the perception of the students included. It was their willingness and confidence to take part in the session that evaluated well. They had identified at the end their surprise at being able to discuss the subject in such detail and with such authority. They noted how surprised they were at their own knowledge base. They also identified how they were able to use the reflective skills within the discussions, bringing theory and practice together.

The other perspectives in this incident include the lecturer's and the university's perception of the curriculum. The lecturer's perception of the session on this occasion was very positive and resulted in a positive outcome for the students. A problem may however arise in future sessions if the next lecture or session for this group is lead in a different manner. For whatever reason, a future session may take a different approach to that of involving the students and approach these students with a 'jug and mug' method of teaching. To the students this might suggest either that their knowledge is no longer relevant or, that the teacher's values and philosophies are in contrast to the first session. Conflicting feelings may be encountered by the students if following sessions do not value the students' contribution.

This session should not be seen as a 'one off session', it is part of a total course where all modules interact with each other. Therefore the university perception must be taken into account. The students are gaining a qualification within the university and from the national body. There is a set list of criteria and learning outcomes to achieve through this course. For this session these were interlinked and previous knowledge was incorporated from previous learning.

Parts and qualities

Here Tripp suggests we examine our attitudes, values and judgements in relation to the incident. This can be done from the lecturer's point in relation to the values behind teaching practice, the approach that we attempt with our students and the manner in which this teaching is carried out. Why are we attempting to teach what some people may see as a clinical skills subject and what are we expecting the student to get out of further study within an academic establishment? This relates directly to our philosophy of teaching. Why we enter into the role in the first place, what we expect as teachers to get out of it and what we expect our students to gain from the experience. Viewing our own values in relation to teaching can help us identify why and how we approach the role and identify our attitudes towards the students and their learning. It is our belief that the teaching done within the classroom will ultimately affect patient care by improving the knowledge base of the students, making them more critical thinkers and reflective practitioners in their own approach to the clinical work.

Learning is seen as a shared experience focused around the learner. Self-directed learning, as described by Knowles (1975), involves the students identifying their own needs, learning objectives and criteria for evaluation, and pursuing learning resources and strategies. Glen (1995) suggests that this teaching within higher education establishments is a process of freeing the mind and bringing about a level of self-empowerment in the individual student. Arguably one of the purposes of education is to achieve certain qualities of mind and attitudes and feelings. This was attempted and successful in this incident with the students. Stenhouse (1975) notes that the curriculum is an attempt to communicate the essential principles and features of an educational proposal in such a form that it is open to critical scrutiny and capable of effective translation into practice. However, as identified by Wong (1979), students need to be committed to the belief that facts in the classroom study are pertinent to other situations. Here again, the authors felt that the students noted the value of their discussion directly to their specialist area of care.

Reversal

Here Tripp talks about viewing the situation from the opposite point of view. This turns justification for in-action into questions and answers. Some of our basic dilemmas with regard to teaching decisions, become a very powerful form of challenge.

This can be addressed in relation to the course curriculum and our values and beliefs as lecturers, the institution in relation to its regulations and, in this situation, to the English National Board who accredit this programme as part of a professional registration. Each person or organisation has their own agenda in relation to taught matter within the course and all must be incorporated into the programme. They may all agree with the approach to adult learning within identified parameters, however, they are all identifying their own set criteria in relation to learning outcomes within the curriculum of the programme. For example, the English National Board identify the time for practice verses theory input and the university identifies the teaching and learning strategy for the programme. Both have their own assessment regulations and it is the responsibility of the lecturer to address each of these through the delivery of the programme.

The approach used must then be justified by all aspects and the identification of a competent practitioner at a higher level of practice must be achieved.

Omissions

This aspect asks us to identify what we have left out rather than stopping once we have analysed the subject. It creates another level of reflection and analysis on the incident. If the programme is viewed as a whole, then both pedagogical and androgogical approaches work together. For the session in question, the ability to reflect and discuss would not have been possible if the students were not so far into their programme and had met a variety of approaches to learning. The pedagogical approach to learning had been utilised in other sessions when introducing new subject matter. Each lecturer needs to be able to justify their teaching styles and strategies. If the students are experienced and experts in their field then a more androgogical approach might be more appropriate. There are no blueprints here. We all learn in different ways and have different approaches to learning. Wong (1979) suggests that we need to be mindful of those students who might retain information in a meaningful manner from a lecture session but subsequently are not able to transfer and apply this knowledge to actual clinical work. For this reason, the programme and total course constantly uses reflection to draw on the experience of the students and allow them to relate the knowledge directly to their clinical area. The programme's learning outcomes must be fulfilled within the module outline for the student to complete their assignment and gain the award.

Conclusion

The ability to assume responsibility for one's own learning is essential to ongoing professional development (Iwasiw, 1987) and this was demonstrated by the students throughout this session. The outcomes of this reflective analysis of an incident highlighted several issues for the authors including the group's ability to reflect on their practice and appreciate the relevant interactions between theory and practice. The student's willingness to participate in the session and value the opinions of their peers was also reflected in the evaluation of the session.

Some argue that reflection is a particular form of thinking (Ghaye and Lillyman, 2000). Critical thinking is therefore an important attribute of the reflective process. Tripps' work helps us to think through the significance of such incidents. It can help lead to a greater understanding or 'conscientization' as defined by Freire (1972), not only for the student in reflecting on their roles but also for the authors in understanding how reflection can facilitate a very positive moment within the classroom.

References

Benner P (1984) *From Novice to Expert: Excellence and Power in Clinical Nursing.* Addison Wesley, Menlo Park, CA

Bernstein B (1977) *Class, Codes and Control. Vol 3 Towards a theory educational transmission.* Routledge and Kegan Paul, London

Condells S, Elliot N (1989) Gayne's Theory of Instruction — Its Relevance to Nurse Education. *Nurse Ed Today* **9**: 281–284

de Bono E (1987) *The CoRT Thinking Course.* Pergamon, London

Freire P (1972) *Pedagogy of the Oppressed.* Penguin, Harmondsworth

Gagne RM (1985) *The Conditions of Learning.* 4th edn. Holt Saunders International Editions, New York

Ghaye T, Lillyman S (1999) *Learning Journals and Critical Incidents.* Quay Books, Mark Allen Publishing Ltd, Dinton, Salisbury, Wiltshire

Ghaye T, Lillyman S (2000) *Reflection: Principles and Practice for Healthcare Professionals.* Quay Books, Mark Allen Publishing Ltd, Dinton, Salisbury, Wiltshire

Glen S (1995) Towards a New Model of Nursing Education. *Nurse Ed Today* **15**: 90–95

Iwasiw C (1987) The Role of the Teacher in Self Directed Learning. *Nurse Ed Today* **7**: 222–7

Knowles M (1975) *Self Directed Learning.* Follett Publishing, Chicago

Laycock A, Munro P (1966) *Educational Psychology.* Pitman and Sons Ltd, London

Lillyman S (1999) Assessing Competence. In: Castledine G, McGee P (eds) (1999) *Specialist and Advanced Nursing Practice.* Blackwell Science, Oxford

Pendleton S (1991) Curriculum Planning in Nursing Education: towards the year 2000. In: Pendleton S, Myles A (eds) *Curriculum Planning In Nurse Education, Practical Applications.* Edward Arnold, London

Reed J, Procter S (1993) *Nurse Education — A reflective approach.* Edward Arnold, London

Rogers J (1989) *Adult Learning.* 3rd edn. OU Press, Milton Keynes

Stenhouse L (1975) *An Introduction to Curriculum Research and Development.* Heinemann, London

Tripp D (1993) *Critical Incidents and Teaching, Developing Professional Judgement.* Routledge, London

United Kingdom Central Council for Nursing, Midwifery and Health Visiting (1990) *The Report of Post-registration Education and Practice Project.* UKCC, London

Whittle T (1999) *Curriculum Development as an Action Research Approach: The Nurse Educator as an Advanced Nurse Practitioner.* Unpublished MSc Thesis, University of Central England, Birmingham

Wong J (1979) The Inability to Transfer Classroom Learning to Clinical Nursing Practice: A learning problem and its remedial plan. *J Adv Nurs* **4**: 161–168

7

A caring moment with Margaret

Helen Taylor

The caring moment

My previous encounters with Margaret had been brief. I had dashed in and out of her room on many occasions. I would hand her first her pills, and then a glass of water poured from the jug on the table beside her chair. Usually I would stand as she took each tablet individually, gulping mouthfuls of water to swill them down. I would often ask the same questions: 'How are you today?' 'Do you want your curtains opened?' And then make an appropriate comment on the weather 'Oh, its a lovely/sunny/ windy/wet/frosty day today'. I would then take the glass from her hand, replace it on the table, and repeat the process with the resident in the next room. The drug rounds were large and took a long time. Some of the residents had problems swallowing. Others were confused and could easily become frightened or aggressive if they were not treated with the utmost care.

I was working as a RN in a large nursing home. On the morning shift I would have charge of one of the two floors, twenty-two residents and three care assistants. On an afternoon shift I would have sole charge of the entire home of forty-four residents and six care assistants. I was always very busy. 'I'll come back later' and 'someone will be along to help you in a moment' were oft repeated phrases as I dashed around changing dressings, administering drugs and checking on residents that care assistants had expressed concern about. I spent time with relatives, answering telephone queries and assessing residents that had fallen. I had a responsibility for the total care of some very elderly, dependent and vulnerable people.

These people were not in hospital; this was their home. Some of them had been resident for many years. We celebrated their birthdays and mourned their deaths. In many cases we became closely involved with their families. They shared news of births and exam successes, but we avoided involvement in the inevitable arguments and disputes. Relatives often experienced feelings of guilt. They felt that putting their parent in a home was the ultimate act of betrayal. These sons or daughters needed a lot of reassurance and support. They usually coped by spending as much time as possible with their parent, and could be very critical of the care they received. The work was very emotionally and physically demanding.

Margaret had been resident for two years, admitted because she was no longer able to cope at home. She suffered from chronic depression, and had also had a C.V.A. several years previously which had left her with a left-sided weakness. She was no longer able to walk, even aided.

On several occasions I had been called to Margaret's room because she had been discovered lying on the floor. It was generally accepted that Margaret placed herself on the floor deliberately, sometimes with quite devastating results. On a number of occasions she had been witnessed easing her body from the chair, pushing the table out of the way beforehand. Despite receiving psychiatric support and anti-depressants, Margaret continued to inflict sometimes serious injuries on herself. This was something the staff found difficult to cope with.

Some of the care assistants considered her to be 'bell-happy'. Each time a resident rang their nurse call bell it was logged by a computerised system. On a number of occasions Margaret had been found to ring her bell in excess of fifty times in a six-hour period. On days such as these, the staff would lose patience with her. Often when asked how they could help her, Margaret would either not reply or say that she did not know. It was difficult to know how to help.

On this particular morning, I had given Margaret her morning pills as I had many times before. We were, as usual, extremely busy. One of the agency staff had not arrived for her shift. After I had completed the drug round, I fed Mary a bowl of porridge and a cup of tea. The residents had breakfast in their own rooms, so we dashed around collecting the trays. I collected Margaret's. The night shift often dressed her but, on this occasion, had not. She was sat in an upright armchair facing out into the corridor, a thick, pink velour dressing gown draped around her shoulders. Her thin face was a mass of bruises, scars and scabs. I knew that her arms and legs had a similar appearance. She looked at me. She had Cornflakes encrusted around her mouth, and tea had dribbled down her chin. More Cornflakes were littered on the table and on her clothes. 'Please Sister', she pleaded. 'I'm wet.'

At this point I looked at the photographs on her chest of drawers. I had seen them many times, this time a familiar face grabbed my attention. Familiar, but not the same. Beautifully styled hair, impeccably applied cosmetics. No Cornflakes, tea, *bruises scabs or scars. This was a face full of joy and optimism, gazing into the eyes of a man she obviously loved very much. Not the face full of humiliation and despair before me now. I put down the tray that I was holding and put my arms around her shoulders. I experienced a feeling of deep warmth for this deeply unhappy lady. She seemed to enjoy the contact. I asked her if she would like a bath. She nodded.*

I assured Margaret that I would be back very soon. I gave my staff a hurried report on any changes to the residents' conditions overnight, and then made allocations. Although there was a named nurse system, it was often impossible to operationalise because of staff shortages and turnover. Within five minutes people were scurrying in all directions, collecting the last of the trays and then going to prepare the residents for the day.

I hurried back to Margaret's room, having started to run a bath on the way. I knocked on the closed door and entered. I transferred her into a wheelchair and then positioned her in front of the wardrobe. I opened the door. 'What would you like to wear today?' I asked. She looked at me mutely. 'OK then, would you like trousers or a skirt?' 'Skirt', she answered. I then hunted through the wardrobe until Margaret had selected her outfit, a pleated beige skirt and a cream, lace trimmed blouse. She opted to take a beige cardigan with us to the bathroom, and decide then whether to wear it or not. Margaret was not enthusiastic when I asked if she wanted to take any toiletries, but I took some anyway.

In the bathroom she agreed to having some bubble bath put in the water. As the room filled with steam and the bath filled with rose scented foam, I gently peeled off her urine soaked clothes. 'They didn't come', she said 'I asked them but they didn't come'. I bent and looked into her eyes, once bright and clear, now opaque with cataracts, and blurred with tears . 'I am sorry', I said. I really was. I helped her onto the toilet, and giving her the bell cord, went to wait outside. Everywhere around me there was activity. The domestic vented some frustration on the carpet as she hoovered. Care assistants rushed around with arms full of towels. Bells rang. An unmistakable smell of urine escaped from some of the rooms. The bell rang. I knocked and went back into the bathroom.

I tested the temperature of the water before I helped Margaret into the bath. It felt fine, but she asked for a little more cold to be added. I did so, and then asked her to hold on to the handles while I reclined the Parker bath. Once she had adjusted to the sensation of the warm water covering her body, Margaret visibly seemed to relax. I asked her if she would like the whirlpool on. She nodded. Not all of the residents like the sensation of the water bubbling around them, but most seem to find it very soothing. I gave Margaret a cloth and held the soap for her, and she began to wash, careful not to knock off the scabs. Such gentleness seemed to be at odds with the fact that she had inflicted those injuries on herself.

I sat on a chair next to the bath. I asked her if she had ever worked. In a quiet, stuttering voice she told me about the Second World War. She had been a nurse and had worked overseas with the forces. I was surprised as there was no mention of this in her notes and no one had told me that Margaret had been a nurse. All the time she was talking, she stared into my eyes. I was close enough for her to see. Sometimes this can feel uncomfortable, disconcerting, but I felt that Margaret needed to know that I was really listening.

Margaret had met her husband towards the end of the war. He had been widowed and left with three young children. He had wooed her and whisked her off her feet. He was the love of her life. They were wealthy and lived a comfortable life. She became stepmother to his children. They had resented her, and never fully accepted her. At this point, I recalled a rather anxious looking middle aged woman that came to visit Margaret most weekends. She seemed to care and always showed an interest in how Margaret was. I asked Margaret about her. She told me that she was her stepdaughter and that they had got on quite well. Her two stepsons, however, had never really seemed to like her. Margaret's big regret was that she had never had children of her own. She had tried to love her husband's children as her own. He had not wanted any more. Her husband had had a fatal heart attack almost twenty years ago. The children had left home and Margaret was alone. She had a lot of friends, she told me, but it was not the same.

'I'm getting cold', said Margaret. I finished washing her feet, and then raised the bath back into an upright position. I wrapped her battered body in warm, fluffy towels. She looked sad, and I felt sad that a person should feel so much pain that they could inflict even more on themselves. I gently dried her and dressed her. She agreed to have some perfume and lipstick on, and decided that she would have her cardigan on. I handed her the comb. She was careful not to disturb the scabs on her scalp. I gathered her things together and wheeled her back into her room, the scent of roses following us up the corridor.

After I had settled her into her chair she asked me to put the radio on. She could not read anymore, she told me. She was waiting to have her cataracts removed. She greatly enjoyed reading and missed it. How did she fill her day? Before I left the room, I stood back and looked at her. She looked comfortable in her chair, with a rug tucked around her legs. Her bed was made, the room was tidy and the early spring sunlight glistened on an exquisite crystal vase full of daffodils in the window. The light and the lipstick made her face come alive. I told her that she looked lovely, and she smiled. I meant it; she was a beautiful woman.

Some of my reflections on this caring moment

I reflected on this caring moment during my coffee break later that morning intuitively drawing upon my understanding of reflection. Initially, I simply felt satisfaction that I had helped to make Margaret physically comfortable. I had spent time with her, listened to her and treated her with respect and helped to maintain her dignity. I felt that I had 'connected' with her, developed an understanding of who and what she was. This eighty-five year old lady had led a full life before she became old and dependent upon others for almost every aspect of living. She was educated, had travelled and experienced the world. She had loved and been loved.

This interaction has had a significant effect on my professional practice and on me personally. Why? I had worked in several nursing homes and had worked with many elderly people. I remember most of them, but I believe that Margaret has had the greatest impact on me. I have thought about that time we spent together many times, wondering if I had really helped her, what I had done well and how I could have helped her more. Margaret made me acknowledge and confront theories and ideologies, challenge my own approach to nursing and how I teach junior staff. It helped me to clarify expectations of myself and others.

Holistic care had been the main ethos of my undergraduate nurse training, and was one that I had thought that I incorporated into my professional practice. I wanted to know my residents, to understand them. When caring for the elderly I attempt to remember that the small, wasted being that I am feeding is an individual who has experienced far more life than I have. They have lived through a war, maybe two. They have cooked meals, managed budgets, planted vegetables and perhaps given birth. They have known pain and hardship, joy and triumph. They have splashed through puddles in the rain and slipped on ice.

I felt ashamed that for a long time with Margaret I had not really seen this. I had spent time with her in the past, but she had been unresponsive to me. Unfortunately, I allowed this to shape my perception of her. Why had it been a surprise to me that she had been a nurse, was well travelled and educated? Possibly because I was afraid of the commitment of getting to know her and why she was in so much emotional pain. I used the excuse of being too busy because if I knew the truth then I would have to deal with it.

Gibson (1994) suggested that by 'allowing' an older person to reminisce, a carer is reversing roles. They are receiving a gift of knowledge from a person who is used to being the recipient of care. This may help improve the older person's feeling of self-worth. By discussing their past they are reviewing their life. This may help to put their current situation into perspective. I was pleased that Margaret felt able to talk to me. I have talked to her again about her nursing career. It is terrible to think about the wealth of knowledge and experience that dies when a person does. I encourage care assistants to talk to the residents. They have made some quite surprising discoveries.

When I had told the care assistants that I would be bathing Margaret that morning they had said 'good'. She was not a popular resident. I must confess that I would not usually have volunteered to dress her. Her physical appearance was threatening, evidence of our failure to help her. She was demanding and needy.

Staff responses to Margaret may be considered in the context of Stockwell's (1972) definition of the 'unpopular patient'. She proposed that individuals operating within a discrete situation may be considered to be a 'group' and that, as such, the members would be bound by 'laws that govern the behaviour of people in small social groups'. These are either implicit or explicit. Those members of the group who do not conform to these laws or rules, for whatever reason, will be considered by the others to be 'deviant'. Deviance will almost invariably result in the offending individual becoming unpopular with other group members. Residents and staff may be considered members of a group. They are living and working in the same organisation. Rules are essential for the effective operation of this organisation.

Some of the care assistants thought that Margaret was selfish; dominating their time. When she rang her bell they would often have to leave the resident they were with to attend to her. She was breaking the rules. This frustrated them, they wanted to provide good care to all the residents, not just the demanding few.

I thought about my own responses to Margaret in the past. If called to her after she had fallen I would be worried that she had hurt herself. I would check her for fractures, cuts and bruising. I would talk to her, ask why she had done it. Did I really want to know? I would attempt to comfort her. But, at the back of my mind would be the thought that I now had a lot of paperwork to complete; accident forms and so on. I would sense the irritation of the care assistants as they stood behind me, hands on hips. They may have had to interrupt feeding someone to tend, yet again to Margaret. This illustrates the point made by Millar (1990) that perceptions of what is difficult or deviant behaviour are subjective, often dependent on the situation within which the behaviour occurs, and who is involved. When staff were less busy Margaret was more likely to be treated sympathetically. Some staff were naturally more inclined to empathise with Margaret than others.

Ferry (1994) reported on an operant/respondent hypothesis, that in some individuals depression may lead to self-harm, and that the harm would reduce for a time the feeling of depression. The cycle is therefore self-reinforcing. At times of depression the person will self-harm. The greater the depression the greater the physical harm. A physical pain to alleviate an emotional pain. A positive feedback mechanism. An awareness of what they are doing to themselves physically, may well make the individual feel more wretched, it certainly will not make them feel better. Although my words were sympathetic, I am sure that if Margaret had been aware of our negative body language, it cannot have helped resolve her emotional pain.

Murray (1998) suggested that there is often little nurses can do to prevent self-harm. The individual needs support and people to understand that they are harming themselves to cope with their distress. He proposed that to understand their suffering, caregivers should not suppress their subjectivity. They must not, however, be judgmental, either verbally or non-verbally. Harrison (1998) stated that these people need understanding and empathy, and should not be dismissed as manipulative. We need to examine our own attitudes and prejudices. During that time in the bathroom with Margaret, we were able to communicate effectively. I saw, in part, why she was so unhappy. She felt that her life was empty, sad and lonely. The anti-depressants did not take that emotional pain away. Nothing could, but perhaps some empathetic support would make her feel a little less alone, more valued as a person.

One can only imagine how it feels to go from being independent and self-determining to being wholly dependent on strangers for everything. Margaret is continent but unable to walk. In order to get to the toilet she needed someone to respond to her call bell. Sometimes, if staff were busy, she would wait and wait, and then perhaps wet herself. This upsets me. It is difficult to acknowledge that a person who has full bladder control may have incontinence imposed upon them.

Allen (1996) described the distressing situation a hospitalised elderly relative found herself in. She had requested to use the bedpan at mealtime, only to be told that she would have to wait until the meal was over because of the risk of cross-infection. On a couple of occasions this poor lady had wet the bed. She experienced a feeling of great embarrassment. I am sure that all nurses can recall an occasion when they have asked someone to wait 'just a moment'. I can. Imagine how you would feel if you were sitting in a lecture, for example, and were forbidden to leave the room after having been given a large dose of diuretics. You tried to control it, but could not, and wet yourself.

A study by Patterson (1995) investigated the process of residents settling into nursing home life. Moving away from familiar surroundings into what is essentially an institutional setting, is a very stressful experience. Patterson examined new residents' perceptions of what staff behaviours they considered to be supportive and non-supportive. Physical assistance, such as being helped into the bath and having call bells responded to promptly rated highly on the supportive behaviours. A lack of sympathy for the effects of ageing; a display of negative attitudes to the resident, and a failure for staff to show concern or respect were identified as non-supportive.

If we have needs it is easier to cope with them if they are dealt with efficiently. Imagine if you had gone to a restaurant for a meal. You had to stand, awkwardly, for five minutes before you could attract a waiter's attention. You were then seated and left. You had no cutlery. No one offered you a drink. Again you had to try and attract the waiter's attention. 'Ok, Ok,' he said, and stood shuffling from one foot to the other while you attempted to order your food. It arrived after rather a long wait. The waiter disappeared before you could remind him that you had no cutlery. You would probably feel very uncomfortable about summoning this unhelpful character again. By the time you got to eat your meal it was cold. If you were assertive, you would have complained. If you lacked confidence or self-esteem you may not have complained. You did not enjoy your meal. You would not go to that restaurant again. You did not feel valued as a customer or as a person. It almost goes without saying that you would have enjoyed your meal in a restaurant where the service was good and where the staff anticipated your needs.

Burnard (1997) expresses the view that we care for others because we must. He puts it another way by saying that we are able to reflect on our own humanity and we are able to recognise the humanity of others. He presses the point by arguing that once we realise that the world is peopled with creatures like ourselves, we feel (or should feel) the need to treat those 'others' as we would want to be treated ourselves.

This is something that I identify strongly with. I felt pleased that I had given Margaret the opportunity to select her clothes. Our choice of clothing is an expression of how we feel about ourselves. Some days I want to look smart, others I just want to feel comfortable. But how I dress is an inherent part of me. Why should I presume to choose Margaret's clothes when she was capable of doing this for herself? There is little opportunity for choice in nursing home life. Meals are at the same time each day, and the daily routine tends to be structured around them. I therefore think that it is important to be flexible whenever possible. Little things can mean a lot, for example, I think Margaret was quite pleased to be asked whether or not she wanted a bubble bath.

Sometimes when I knock on residents' doors they will say, 'oh, you do not need to do that'. But I think that I do. Their room is their home, their sanctuary, and their own personal space. I believe that this gesture conveys my respect for the person and their very limited privacy. Staff are often uncomfortable with having residents' room doors closed, they worry that the resident will perhaps fall or come to some other harm and not be seen. That is a valid argument, but I believe that we all have the right to be on our own, in our own space from time to time, and not be worried that someone is going to walk in without being invited.

Margaret's bell ringing was a cry for help. Yes, she was an attention seeker, but it was attention she deserved and needed. Peplau (1988) identified that all individuals have needs and that if these needs are not fulfilled, then tensions will arise and manifest themselves in a variety of ways. When these needs are fulfilled, then the individual will experience satisfaction. She proposed that,

> *All human behaviour is purposeful and goal seeking in terms of feelings of satisfaction and or/security.*
>
> (Peplau, 1988)

When I entered Margaret's room for the second time that morning, I recognised her need. I touched her. Touch can have a multitude of meanings. Residents are physically handled many times each day. But in this context it was an instinctive gesture to communicate to Margaret that I wanted to listen to her. I had an interest in her and a commitment to help her. Minardi and Riley (1997) suggested that light touch, within an appropriate context, may stimulate catharsis, an expression of emotions. This form of communication may be particularly pertinent with clients such as Margaret who are visually impaired. She did respond positively to this touch. Other people, however, may feel threatened or compromised by touch. The nurse needs to be able to read cues carefully. Margaret did not attempt to withdraw, indeed she visibly relaxed. I had to leave Margaret for a short time, which was regrettable but necessary. She appeared pleased to see me return. The moment was not lost.

I have already declared my own feelings of satisfaction following this interaction with Margaret. I believe that this is important. Jean Watson's *Philosophy and Science of Caring* (1989) explored an humanistic approach to nursing, and the establishment of a trusting interpersonal relationship between nurse and client. She acknowledged that caring is an integral part of nursing, and that effective caring is satisfying for both nurse and client. However, this relationship requires acceptance of both positive and negative feelings and that something may be positive at an emotional level and negative at an intellectual level or vice versa.

On an emotional level I felt satisfaction that I had cared for Margaret, and that our interpersonal relationship would be ongoing. I talked to care assistants and discussed with them their feelings for Margaret. I explained her needs. I reinforced that the residents' privacy should be respected, and that they should be helped to maintain their dignity. If it is safe to do so, residents should be allowed to use the toilet in privacy. They should not be made to feel rushed. Comments should not be made about any odours produced. Generally, the untrained staff were committed to caring. Omissions were usually due to a gap in their training. They were motivated to learn.

On an intellectual level though, I knew that nothing major had changed for Margaret. People did try, but she would continue to grieve for her lost husband, life and independence. She would continue to suffer the indignity of needing someone else to take her to the toilet. Her meals would be served at the times prescribed by nursing home routine and generally she would have little choice of what she ate. She would continue to have near strangers walk into her room, sometimes unannounced. She would have people peer at her in the depths of the night to check that she was still breathing. Although she made use of the talking library, until her cataracts were removed she would not be able to read. She could not be persuaded to join in organised activities, or to eat in the dining room. It seemed likely that she would sit, in room twelve, staring into the corridor for the rest of her life.

'Empowerment' is a word frequently used in nursing theory and practice today (Ghaye, Gillespie and Lillyman, 2000). It means different things to different people, but Rodwell's (1996) analysis of the literature concluded that empowerment involves facilitating a client's autonomy. By working to develop their self-esteem and a sense of value, they may be encouraged to take responsibility for their own health and decisions concerning their life. The nurse will need to accept that clients' decisions may have negative affects on their health. We had to provide Margaret with choices and options, but accept and respect her decisions.

I know that the care assistants cared about Margaret, as they cared about all the residents. Their work was very demanding and they were often very short staffed. Several had been working at this home for a number of years and were very dedicated. But when dependency levels and pressures of work are high, staff can become stressed. Bond (1986) suggested that at times like this, care staff might become irritable or lack the patience necessary to care effectively.

Rodwell's (1996) review of the literature, indicated that for a health worker to be able to value her client sufficiently to facilitate empowerment, she needs to respect and value herself and her practice. On reflection, I think that is something to be aware of. Indeed, some of my analysis makes me feel uncomfortable. I sound judgmental and uncaring, make excuses for myself. Perhaps at times I could have been more understanding, have tried harder to relate to some of the residents. But I am a caring nurse. The well being of my clients is the basis of my practice, and I communicate concerns about the organisation to the management team. Ongoing education of the care staff, and increased management support at times of stress may improve their sense of worth. They need to know that they are valued and that they are doing a good job.

Research by Sumaya-Smith (1995) indicated that close inter-personal relationships between care staff and residents was integral to staff retention. These 'surrogate family bonds' require considerable emotional investment by staff, but are greatly valued by staff and residents. I can identify with this. Although my relationship with Margaret has no history, it is ongoing. This is a privilege, and the reason I chose to work in a nursing home. My caring moment with Margaret was a clarifying moment. I enjoy working with elderly people, getting to know them and maybe making a real difference to their later years. I have been able to recognise that at times factors may threaten and hinder this.

Through reflecting on my practice in this chapter I feel that I am now in a much stronger position to provide, and to help others provide, the care that these people deserve.

References

Allen J (1996) A Time And A Place. *Nurs Standard* **10**(17): 49

Bond M (1986) *Stress And Self-Awareness: A Guide For Nurses.* Heinemann Nursing, Oxford

Burnard P (1997) Why care? Ethical And Spiritual Issues In Caring Nursing. In: Brykczynska G (ed) (1997) *Caring. The Compassion And Wisdom Of Nursing.* Edward Arnold, London

Ferry R (1994) Complex Causes. *Nurs Times* **90**(3): 34–5

Ghaye T, Gillespie D, Lillyman S (2000) *Empowerment through Reflection: The Narratives of Healthcare Professionals.* Quay Books, Mark Allen Publishing Ltd, Dinton, Salisbury, Wiltshire

Gibson F (1994) *Reminiscence And Recall: A Guide To Good Practice.* Age Concern England, London

Harrison A (1998) A Harmful Procedure. *Nurs Times* **94**(27): 37–8

Millar R (1990) *Managing Difficult Patients.* Faber and Faber, London

Minardi HA, Riley MJ (1997) *Communication In Health Care: A Skills Based Approach.* Butterworth-Heinemann, Oxford

Murray I (1998) At The Cutting Edge. *Nurs Times* **94**(27): 37–7

Patterson BJ (1995) The Process Of Social Support: Adjusting To Life In A Nursing Home. *J Adv Nurs* **21**: 682–689

Peplau H (1988) *Interpersonal Relations In Nursing.* MacMillan, London

Rodwell CM (1996) An Analysis Of The Concept Of Empowerment. *J Adv Nurs* **23**: 305–313

Stockwell F (1972) *The Unpopular Patient.* Royal College Of Nursing, London

Sumaya-Smith I (1995) Caregiver/Resident Relationships: Surrogate Family Bonds and Surrogate Grieving in a Skilled Nursing Facility. *J Adv Nurs* **21**: 447–451

Watson J (1989) Philosophy And Science Of Caring. In: Marriner-Tomey A (ed) (1989) *Nursing Theorists And Their Work*. CV Mosby Company, St Louis

8
Dehumanising caring moments?

Jo Hamilton-Jones

What follows stands in sharp contrast to the qualitative accounts of practice presented earlier. In this chapter, I am going to illustrate how information technology (IT) can be used to enhance reflection. The main goal is to show how IT can help us to understand certain clinical situations more clearly, deeply and richly. In other words, to make more sense of them so that we can perhaps act more effectively, confidently and safely. In order to gain the most from this chapter, we first need to become familiar with the key ideas of modelling and simulation. Brace yourself. The language used is different from the first person reflections in earlier chapters. It will challenge you. It is a different way of seeing and understanding.

The process of modelling and simulation lies at the centre of many methods of computer analysis (Rothery, 1990). The idea of modelling can be understood for example with regard to a flight simulator. The simulation is made to be as realistic as possible in order to understand the nature of flying, the complex decisions that need to be made and all in a context of lots of things happening at once and unpredictably. The simulation can also help us to reflect-in-action, think on our feet and resolve problems and difficulties as they arise. It is not only the flying operation which is modelled. The effect of the weather on the plane is being modelled too. This system includes many of the features of reality that influence the progress and outcome of the situation.

We can use modelling in an investigative way in healthcare, particularly when the user is trying to understand something better in order to make more rational, planned and principled decisions. One kind of modelling, called spreadsheet modelling, can help us develop our skilfulness in the decision-making process. Among other functions the computer can be used to carry out some mathematical computations. Using a spreadsheet enables complicated analyses to be undertaken without getting into time-consuming and complicated calculations.

This chapter illustrates one of the many uses of information technology. It simulates some real-life situations which will be familiar to a number of healthcare professionals. The first simulation is called 'the doctor's waiting room'. In order to achieve the aims stated above I have tried to help us see it differently and to think again about it by applying a well-known mathematical queueing problem. I then go on to develop the idea of modelling and simulation and how it can help us in our healthcare work by drawing on more complex situations which, for example, could occur in a hospital department. This chapter is not intended to be a completely definitive solution to such problems. Rather the intention is to show how IT can be used to help us to reflect on practice, encourage ideas and inspire confidence to be creative in the resolution of everyday problems. In this sense IT is an invaluable aid to reflective practices.

Doctor's waiting room — no appointments

In 1962, the Operational Research Society and the Ministry of Health arranged a discussion on the subject of appointment systems in hospitals and general practice. One of the papers dealt with the design of an appointments system for a GP's morning surgery, which ran theoretically from 9am to 11am. Before the appointment system, patients began to arrive at about 8am and a queue of up to ten people had usually formed by the time the surgery doors were opened at 8.30am. By 9am, the queue had increased to up to thirty people, overflowing the waiting room. This, together with the fact that the doctor was often late, meant that patients had to wait a very long time — about an hour and a half on average.

The paper considered a GP working on his own. In 'queueing language', this is a single service station with a 'first come, first served' queue discipline.

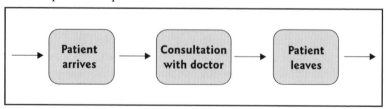

Figure 8.1: A doctor's waiting room model

Although this model could be considered to be relatively 'simple' in today's real-life scenarios, it provides a suitable starting position for the analysis.

To continue the analysis, in order to specify such a system, we need to know:

* the distribution (pattern) of the doctor's consulting time
* the nature of the arrival pattern of the patients.

From the 800 observations collected in 1962, the work was developed further (Lighthill, 1978) and *Table 8.1* and *Figure 8.2* show the resulting percentage frequency distribution.

Table 8.1: Results from data collection in 1962		
Length of consultation time in minutes	**Average length of consultation time in minutes**	**Percentage of patients with each consulting time**
0.5–1.499	1	10
1.5–2.499	2	16
2.5–3.499	3	18
3.5–4.499	4	16
4.5–5.499	5	12
5.5–6.499	6	10
6.5–7.499	7	6
7.5–8.499	8	4
8.5–9.499	9	3
9.5–10.499	10	2
10.5–11.499	11	0
11.5–12.499	12	0
12.5–13.499	13	0
13.5–14.499	14	0
14.5–15.499	15	0
15.5–16.499	16	1
16.5–17.499	17	0
17.5–18.499	18	0
18.5–19.499	19	2
19.5–20.499	20	0

For ease of calculation, some approximations have been made; any consulting times occurring between 2.5 mins and 3.499 mins were allocated the consulting time of 3. From *Table 8.1* and *Figure 8.2*, we can see that the majority of the appointments lasted less than ten minutes with the average consulting time of 4.55 minutes per patient. *Table 8.1* also highlights the percentage of patients associated with each consultation length. In statistical terms, this could be described as the 'percentage frequency'. These results provide the structure or 'frequency distribution' on which to base the simulation.

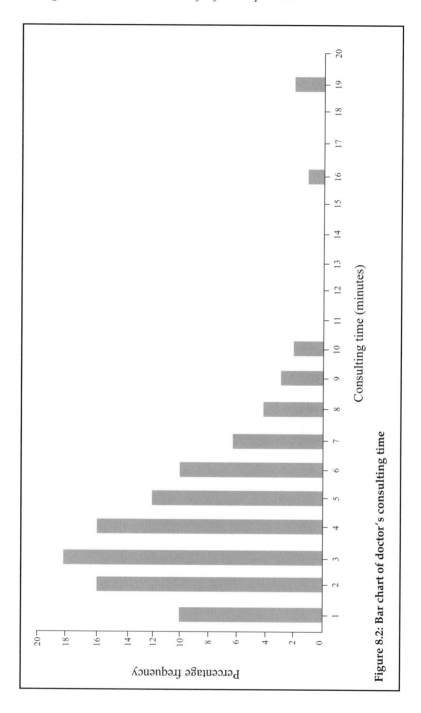

Figure 8.2: Bar chart of doctor's consulting time

Doctors waiting room — appointment system

Consider the situation if an appointment system was implemented. Patients would arrive at prescribed and preferably regular intervals. The object of the exercise would be to determine the best value of the interval between appointments. However, secondary factors are also of interest, eg. the time that patients spend waiting to see the doctor, the time doctors spend waiting for patients to arrive, ie. the time between one patient leaving and the next patient arriving.

Let us say that we want to reflect on the effect of changing the patient inter-arrival interval and the effect this has on the average time patients spend waiting to see the doctor and the total time that the doctor spends waiting to start a consultation. If this is our intention the next task is to generate a simulation, which will enable us to compare the results for different appointment times. In order to make the simulation as lifelike as possible, we need to build the simulated pattern of consultation times around original, empirical (real-world) data. In this case, we shall use the data from *Table 8.1*. However, real-life data can be collected more fitting to a particular situation and adapted accordingly.

Appointments are often scheduled for regular time intervals. We need to be able to experiment to determine which time interval would provide the best possible service for the patient and the doctor. As an initial attempt, let us consider the situation where appointments are scheduled every four minutes, ie. for a surgery starting at 9.00am the appointments would be made for 9.00am, 9.04am, 9.08am, 9.12am and so on. In 'queueing' terminology, we call this an 'inter-arrival time' of four minutes.

Now we want to simulate the length of the consultation process. We have assumed here that each patient arrives at the surgery at the scheduled time of their appointment. In real-life of course we know that this is not always the case. However, this assumption was made at this stage in order to keep the analysis as straightforward as possible. The start of each consultation will be affected by the finishing time of the previous consultation. If the patient arrives at the surgery, given the assumptions above, and the doctor is free, then the consultation can start immediately. However, if the patient arrives and previous consultation(s) are still underway, then the patient has to wait.

From the earlier data collection, we know that there is a pattern in the length of consulting times. The aim here is to generate a similar pattern and thereby produce a simulation that behaves in a very similar manner. We do this by generating a series of random numbers and then 'fit' these into the distribution or pattern developed before.

Some basic spreadsheet information

At this stage, we need to start using a spreadsheet to 'build' the simulation model. It is worth devoting some time here to provide a brief explanation of spreadsheet terms. Spreadsheet software creates a worksheet consisting of rows and columns. The rows are numbered 1, 2, 3…. and the columns are identified by letters, A, B, C.... with double letters used beyond the twenty-sixth column. The intersection of a row and column is called a cell. A cell is identified by a cell reference or cell address, which consists of the column letter followed by the row number.

A user can enter three types of information into a cell in a worksheet. One is a number, another is text and another is a formula. In a formula, the user refers to cell references to identify the data in the computation and mathematical symbols to specify what type of computation is to be performed.

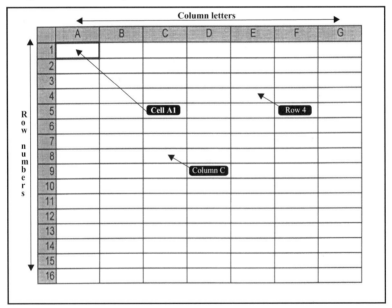

Figure 8.3: An example of a spreadsheet

In this work, I have used EXCEL 97 on a personal computer. There are a considerable number of pre-programmed formulae within this version of EXCEL. I have used certain functions, for example LOOKUP, RAND(), SUM, IF, MAX and LARGE. Further explanations of these terms are included in the following text. In addition, there are special HELP facilities within the package. Although the text of this chapter refers to the use of EXCEL, the simulations which follow could be built on other types of computers with alternative spreadsheet packages.

Using a spreadsheet to build the model

Table 8.2 is formed from the last two columns of *Table 8.1*. This forms the distribution or pattern for the simulation to be built on. This table could be contained in a separate worksheet or could be placed within the operating worksheet. The frequencies from *Table 8.1* are added together one-by-one to form a 'cumulative' percentage frequency. Associated with each of these results is an average length of each consultation. Random numbers can be generated using several functions. The RAND() function within EXCEL will generate random numbers between 0 and 1, eg. 0.6, 0.54. In order to 'fit' these into a specific pattern, we use the LOOKUP function. An example of this is given in *Table 8.2*.

Table 8.2: LOOKUP table for the doctor's waiting room

	A	B	C
1	Cumulative percentage of	Average consultation	Random number
2	patients with each con-	length	
3	sulting time		
4	0	1	58
5	10	2	
6	26	3	
7	44	4	
8	60	5	
9	72	6	
10	82	7	
11	88	8	
12	92	9	
13	95	10	
14	97	16	
15	98	19	

Using the command:

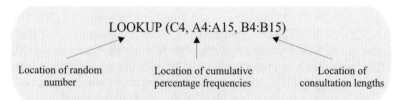

LOOKUP (C4, A4:A15, B4:B15)

Location of random number | Location of cumulative percentage frequencies | Location of consultation lengths

we can search through the data in *Table 8.2* and build up an appropriate 'pattern' of values. As the frequencies are percentages, they lie between 0 and 100 and they will have a total of 100. Consequently, the random numbers need to be generated over the same range. This can be achieved by multiplying each random number by 100.

For example, suppose the random number is 58 in cell C4. The command LOOKUP(C4, A4:A15, B4:B15) would consider the value of C4, which is 58. It would compare it with the values in cells A4, A5, A6... A15 and determine the percentage frequency values which immediately surround the value. In this case, these would be 44 and 60. Each of these values have TIME values associated with them from column B, ie. 4 and 5. The lower of these is taken and the returned value for TIME would be 4.

Table 8.3 (opposite) shows a simulated sequence of events for a two-hour surgery where patients can make appointments at specified four-minute intervals. To provide an insight into the workings of this simulation, let us proceed through the simulation in a step-by-step manner.

Appoint time (column B) represents the time of each appointment. In equation form, this is calculated by adding four to the previous appointment time,

eg. time of appointment = time of previous appointment + 4

Start consult (column C) represents the time that each patient starts their consultation. Towards the beginning of surgery, this is very similar to arrival time. However later in the simulation, as the queue builds up, the value is given by the finishing time of the previous consultation. This is formed using the IF statement in EXCEL.

Consultation start time: if the previous consultation finishes later than the appointment time, then, this consultation starts when the previous consultation finishes. Otherwise, this consultation starts at the scheduled appointment time.

Table 8.3: Simulation of a doctor's waiting room with appointments every four minutes

	A	B	C	D	E	F	G	H
1			Inter-appointment time			4 mins		
2								
3								
4	Patient number	Scheduled appoint. time (mins)	Start time of each con-sultation (mins)	Random number	Length of consulta-tion (mins)	Finish time of each con-sultation (mins)	Doctor's waiting time (mins)	Patient waiting time (mins)
5	1	0	0	66	5	5	0	0
6	2	4	5	85	7	12	0	1
7	3	8	12	10	2	14	0	4
8	4	12	14	26	3	17	0	2
9	5	16	17	7	1	18	0	1
10	6	20	20	6	1	21	2	0
11	7	24	24	53	4	28	3	0
12	8	28	28	28	3	31	0	0
13	9	32	32	49	4	36	1	0
14	10	36	36	89	8	44	0	0
15	11	40	44	1	1	45	0	4
16	12	44	45	85	7	52	0	1
17	13	48	52	36	3	55	0	4
18	14	52	55	85	7	62	0	3
19	15	56	62	33	3	65	0	6
20	16	60	65	57	4	69	0	5
21	17	64	69	25	2	71	0	5
22	18	68	71	6	1	72	0	3
23	19	72	72	82	7	79	0	0
24	20	76	79	65	5	84	0	3
25	21	80	84	56	4	88	0	4
26	22	84	88	23	2	90	0	4
27	23	88	90	62	5	95	0	2
28	24	92	95	88	8	103	0	3
29	25	96	103	11	2	105	0	7
30	26	100	105	94	9	114	0	5
31	27	104	114	98	19	133	0	10
32	28	108	133	96	10	143	0	25
33	29	112	143	19	2	145	0	31
34	30	116	145	39	3	148	0	29
35	31	120	148	93	9	157	0	28
	Average total				4.87096774		6	6.129032

For example, from *Table 8.3* we have:

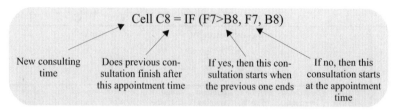

Cell C8 = IF (F7>B8, F7, B8)

New consulting time | Does previous consultation finish after this appointment time | If yes, then this consultation starts when the previous one ends | If no, then this consultation starts at the appointment time

Random number (column D) consists of a sequence of two-digit random numbers, each multiplied by 100, as previously explained .

Length of consultation (column E) represents the time that each consultation lasts. The first random number generated is 66. Using the LOOKUP feature of EXCEL as detailed earlier, this falls within the range of 60–72 of *Table 8.2*, and so the consulting time for the first patient is taken as five minutes. The next random number generated is 85. This falls in the range 82–88 of *Table 8.2*. The consulting time for the second patient is therefore taken as seven minutes.

Doctor's waiting time (column G) represents the length of time that the doctor is kept waiting for each patient to arrive for each consultation. If the finishing time of the previous consultation is less than the start of the next appointment, then the doctor will be kept waiting. This is generated if the previous consultation finishes before the scheduled time of the next appointment.

For example, for cell G10, cell F9 is compared with cell B10. As the value of F9(18) is less than B10(20), this indicates that the doctor had to wait for the next patient. In spreadsheet terms, using *Table 8.3*, this is written as,

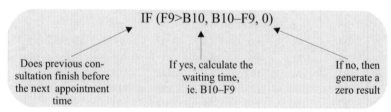

IF (F9>B10, B10–F9, 0)

Does previous consultation finish before the next appointment time | If yes, calculate the waiting time, ie. B10–F9 | If no, then generate a zero result

Patient's waiting time (column H) represents the length of time that each patient is kept waiting to see the doctor. If the finishing time of the previous consultation is greater than the start of the next appointment, then the patient will be kept waiting.

For example, in *Table 8.3*, for cell H7, cell B7 is compared to

C7. As the value of B7, the scheduled appointment time (eight mins), is less than C7, the start of the consultation (12 mins), then the patient has to wait .

In spreadsheet terms, using *Table 8.3*, this is generated from,

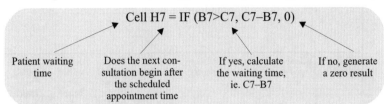

Cell H7 = IF (B7>C7, C7–B7, 0)

| Patient waiting time | Does the next consultation begin after the scheduled appointment time | If yes, calculate the waiting time, ie. C7–B7 | If no, generate a zero result |

The simulation continues for the two-hour period. At the end, it is possible to calculate the average waiting time for the doctor and also for the patient using the AVERAGE function within EXCEL.

One of the main purposes of this simulation is to enable experimentation with several intervals between appointments. For an inter-arrival time of five minutes, *Table 8.4* provides the simulation results over a similar two-hour period.

Running the simulation using several appointment intervals provides the information generated in *Table 8.5*.

Each run of the simulation uses a different set of random numbers. A different set of random numbers produces a different prediction. One spreadsheet is not enough. To see the consequences of the model, the simulation needs to be run several times, each with a different set of random numbers. This way, it will become apparent how long the patients' and doctor's waiting time will vary over time.

This form of simulation would assist in deciding appropriate appointment intervals for a typical doctor's practice where there is one doctor, ie. one service outlet. However, we need to develop the model to try to make it more life-like and therefore more useful.

Table 8.4: Simulation of a doctor's waiting room with appointments every five minutes

	A	B	C	D	E	F	G	H
1			Inter-appointment time			5 mins		
2								
3								
4	Patient number	Scheduled appoint. time (mins)	Start time of each con-sultation (mins)	Random number	Length of consulta-tion (mins)	Finish time of each con-sultation (mins)	Doctor's waiting time (mins)	Patient waiting time (mins)
5	1	0	0	55	4	4	0	0
6	2	5	5	49	4	9	1	0
7	3	10	10	2	1	11	1	0
8	4	15	15	17	2	17	4	0
9	5	20	20	92	9	29	3	0
10	6	25	29	20	2	31	0	4
11	7	30	31	55	4	35	0	1
12	8	35	35	7	1	36	0	0
13	9	40	40	37	3	43	4	0
14	10	45	45	32	3	48	2	0
15	11	50	50	91	8	58	2	0
16	12	55	58	23	2	60	0	3
17	13	60	60	50	4	64	0	0
18	14	65	65	52	4	69	1	0
19	15	70	70	15	2	72	1	0
20	16	75	75	43	3	78	3	0
21	17	80	80	37	3	83	2	0
22	18	85	85	83	7	92	2	0
23	19	90	92	72	6	98	0	2
24	20	95	98	38	3	101	0	3
25	21	100	101	52	4	105	0	1
26	22	105	105	68	5	110	0	0
27	23	110	110	30	3	113	0	0
28	24	115	115	42	3	118	2	0
29	25	120	120	15	2	122	2	0
	Average total				3.68		30.00	0.56

Table 8.5: Comparison of appointment times			
	Average consulting time	Average patient wait time	Total doctor wait time
4 mins	4.87	6.13	6
5 mins	3.68	0.56	30
6 mins	4.55	0.95	28
7 mins	3.78	0.11	55
8 mins	4.75	0.06	53
9 mins	3.79	0.00	67
10 mins	5.77	0.92	50

A hospital scenario — model I

Consider the situation where patients arrive at a hospital for emergency treatment.

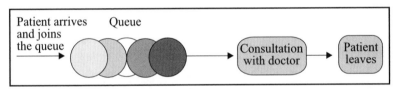

Figure 8.4: Hospital model with one doctor

In this scenario, patients do not have 'fixed' appointment times, ie. they arrive at unspecified intervals. I have used an arrival rate of five, ie. on average, one patient arrives every five minutes and a completion rate of three, ie. on average, one patient takes three minutes to complete their treatment.

Table 8.6: Simulation of accident and emergency department — one doctor

	A	B	C	D	E	F	G
1	Arrival rate		5		Completion rate		3
2							
3	Number of doctors		1				
4							
5	Patient	Time between each arrival (mins)	Arrival of each patient (mins)	Start of each consultation (mins)	Length of each consultation (mins)	Finishing time of each consultation (mins)	Patient waiting time (mins)
6	1	0	0	0	3	3	0
7	2	0	0	3	5	8	3
8	3	2	2	8	2	10	6
9	4	3	5	10	1	11	5
10	5	2	7	11	0	12	4
11	6	1	8	12	2	14	3
12	7	6	14	14	1	15	0
13	8	9	23	23	8	30	0
14	9	1	24	30	1	32	6
15	10	3	27	32	0	32	5
16	11	5	32	32	2	34	0
17	12	8	40	40	4	44	0
18	13	6	46	46	4	51	0
19	14	3	49	51	3	54	1
20	15	0	50	54	3	56	4
21	16	2	52	56	1	57	4
22	17	2	54	57	10	67	3
23	18	5	59	67	3	70	8
24	19	0	59	70	2	72	11
25	20	2	61	72	15	87	11
	Average total	3.21	3.051878		3.57		3.81

Time between each arrival (column B) represents the difference in time between each arrival. In 'queuing terms', this is often referred to as the 'inter-arrival time'.

Patients arrive at 'random'. This means that the probability that a patient arrives at any given instant of time is the same as the probability of an arrival at any other instant of time. This condition implies that the gap between each patient arrival follows a special mathematical pattern, known as the 'exponential probability distribution'. It is therefore likely that the inter-arrival times will be small. The proof of this is outside the scope of this chapter but can be explored by consulting any standard mathematical text. A suitable inter-arrival time can be generated using the formula,

$$- 1 * \text{Arrival rate} * \text{LN(Rand())}$$

The function LN is an EXCEL function. The effect of this is to convert the range of the random number function RAND() from 0 … 1 to the range – (to 0. By multiplying by –1, we obtain a random value in the range 0 to (. Further explanation of this function can be obtained from mathematical texts. However, for this simulation, it is sufficient to know that it is important to use this function to cater for the irregularity of the patient arrivals.

Arrival time (column C) is the time that the next patient arrives. It is formed from the sum of the inter-arrival time and the previous arrival time.

Patient arrival time = Arrival time of previous patient + inter-arrival time

For example, from *Table 8.6*,

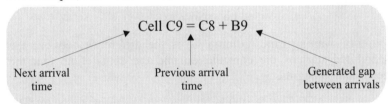

Cell C9 = C8 + B9

Next arrival time   Previous arrival time   Generated gap between arrivals

Start consultation (column D) represents the time that each patient starts their consultation. Towards the beginning of the period, this is very similar to arrival time. However, later in the simulation as the queue builds up, then the value is given by the finishing time of the previous consultation. In equation terms, this is formed using the IF statement in EXCEL,

Consultation start time = If the previous consultation finishes later than the appointment time, then this consultation starts when the previous consultation finishes: otherwise, this consultation starts at the scheduled appointment time, eg. from *Table 8.6*,

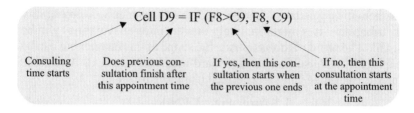

Length of each consultation (column E) is the length of time that each patient spends in consultation with the doctor. This is random (but of course actual or 'real' data can be used) and can be generated in a similar manner to the inter-arrival times (column B). The length of each consultation is generated by the formula,

$$-1 * \text{Completion rate} * \text{LN (RAND())}:$$

Finishing time of each consultation (column F) is given by adding the length of the consultation to the start time of that consultation.

Time consultation finished = Time consultation starts + consultation time

For example, in EXCEL terminology and using *Table 8.6*, this is given by,

$$F9 = D9 + E9$$

Patients' waiting time (column G) is the difference between the scheduled start of the consultation and the actual time that the consultation begins.

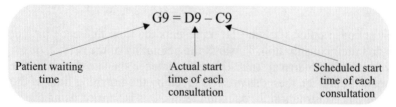

A hospital scenario — model 2

In this particular scenario, I have widened the scope of the previous model (1) to consider the effects of more doctors being available to see incoming patients. In the example below, the patient could see any of three doctors available for consultation.

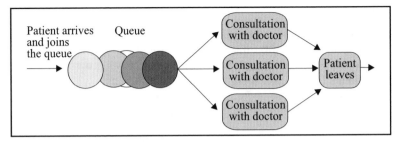

Figure 8.5: Hospital model with three doctors

Table 8.7: Simulation of accident and emergency department — three doctors

	A	B	C	D	E	F	G
1	Arrival rate	5			Completion rate		3
2							
3	Number of doctors		3				
4							
5	Patient	Time between each arrival (mins)	Arrival of each patient (mins)	Start of each consultation (mins)	Length of each consultation (mins)	Finishing time of each consultation (mins)	Patient waiting time (mins)
6	1	0	0	0	3	3	0
7	2	19	19	19	2	21	0
8	3	2	21	21	7	28	0
9	4	14	35	35	2	37	0
10	5	7	42	42	5	47	0
11	6	4	46	46	3	49	0
12	7	3	49	49	3	52	0
13	8	1	50	50	2	52	0
14	9	1	51	51	9	60	0
15	10	1	52	52	5	57	0
16	11	4	56	56	7	63	0
17	12	1	57	57	0	57	0
18	13	1	58	58	1	59	0
19	14	1	59	59	3	62	0
20	15	3	62	62	1	63	0
21	16	14	76	76	1	77	0
22	17	3	79	79	4	83	0
23	18	25	104	104	1	105	0
24	19	5	109	109	6	115	0
25	20	1	110	110	1	111	0
	Average total	5.79	5.5		3.25		0.00

When there are three doctors available, in 'queuing terminology', there are three service outlets. Therefore, for a given client, 'service' can begin either at the time that each patient arrives, or at the third largest finish time for preceding patients (as the other two will still be occupied). In equation form, this can be written as,

Consultation begins: either   if a doctor is available, then the consultation starts immediately

                or   if all the doctors are busy, then the consultation starts when one becomes free

When a patient arrives, any of the three doctors may be available to see them. Alternatively, as there are three doctors available for consultation, we may need to find the third largest value from the previous finishing times to determine the earliest time that one becomes available. As there may be more than one consultation underway at any given moment and the length of each consultation cannot be predicted, then the consultations may not finish in the order that they were started. In short then, what we are moving towards in this chapter is a scenario that may be more, and more realistic. In this sense we have a simulation which has to cope with ever increasing possibilities, uncertainties and probabilities.

Again in equation form we have an alternative way of expressing this. For example,

 Take the largest   either   the current patient arrival time
value of:

                or   third largest previous finishing time

In EXCEL terms, using *Table 8.7*, this can be written as,

Cell D20 = MAX (patient arrival time, third largest from all previous finishing times) = MAX (C20, LARGE (F$6,F19) 3)

In this case, cell D20 is the time that the next consultation is scheduled to start and cell C20 is the arrival time of the patient at the hospital. F$6:F19 are cells showing the finishing times for previous patients and the value three indicates that it is the third largest time that is required within that range. This model can be used for any number of similar 'service' outlets. For example, for five service outlets, we would look for the fifth largest finishing time of the preceding patients. The last parameter of the LARGE function would have the value of five.

Running the simulation several times, varying the number of service outlets available, enables a comparison of results to be made (see *Table 8.8*). It is from such comparisons and reflections on the data, that we can become more informed about alternative and possible courses of action. If reflection is to have a consequence, that is to say lead to some improvements in thinking, practice and the clinical contexts in which it takes place, then using the computer and the appropriate software to generate simulations of this kind, can be an invaluable aid to learning.

Table 8.8: Comparison of the average length of consultation and average patient waiting time using various service areas		
	Average length of consultation	Average patient waiting time
1 doctor	3.57	3.81
2 doctors	2.60	0.04
3 doctors	3.25	0.00
4 doctors	2.05	0.03
5 doctors	3.40	0.00

A hospital scenario — model 3

We can develop this model still further by considering the real-life situation in accident and emergency. In an accident and emergency unit, patients arrive randomly, their condition is assessed and they are treated appropriately, dependent on their condition. This model includes a category for initial diagnosis and also illustrates the use of different service rates to take this into account. The model (*Figure 8.6*) is overleaf.

Here I have made two assumptions: that patients arrive at random and their condition is categorised. Those patients in category 1, designated as the most serious, are treated in one area with the completion rate being adjusted appropriately so as to allow for the consultation time being longer. Those patients in category 2, designated as serious, are treated in another area with a service rate adjusted appropriately so that the simulated consulting times are not quite as long as for category 1. Finally, those patients in category 3, designated as having minor injuries, are seen in another area with a service rate to ensure that the simulation reflects this adjustment and produces shorter consultation times.

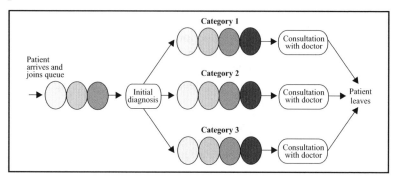

Figure 8.6: Hospital model with three different categories of patient injury

Table 8.9 uses similar formulae to the previous model for inter-arrival time (column B) and arrival time (column C).

Patient type (column D) aims to simulate the random nature of the condition of arrivals. We need to generate random numbers of 1, 2 and 3 to denote the random nature of the severity of injuries. This can be achieved using the EXCEL function, RANDBETWEEN (1, 3). Using this function, categories are allocated randomly to each patient. A development of this model could be to provide specific ratios for these categories to reflect specific trends and provide an even more 'life-like' simulation. For example, 10% category 1 patients, 30% category 2 patients and 60% category 3 patients. Through the use of a LOOKUP table as demonstrated in the doctor's waiting room model, the appropriate values could be simulated.

Table 8.9: Spreadsheet for hospital model with three patient injury categories

	Arrival rate			Very serious Completion rate			5	Serious Completion rate			3	Not serious Completion rate			2
Patient	Time between arrivals	Arrival time	Severity of injury	Patient arrives	Waiting time (mins)	Duration of consult (mins)	Finish time (mins)	Patient arrives	Waiting time (mins)	Duration of consult (mins)	Finish time (mins)	Patient arrives	Waiting time (mins)	Duration of consult (mins)	Finish time (mins)
1	1	1	2				0	1	0	4	5				0
2	3	4	1	4	0	1	5				0				0
3	1	5	1	5	0	20	25				0				0
4	1	6	2				0	6	0	5	11				0
5	1	7	2				0	7	0	4	11				0
6	2	9	1	9	0	0	9				0				0
7	2	11	1	11	0	4	15				0				0
8	1	12	1	15	3	10	25				0				0
9	1	13	2				0	13	0	1	14				0
10	2	15	3				0				0	15	0	1	16
11	1	16	3				0				0	16	0	2	18
12	3	19	3				0				0	19	0	0	19
13	1	20	2				0	13	0	6	26				0
14	1	21	2				0		0	1	22				0
15	2	23	3				0				0	23	0	0	23
16	1	24	1	25	1	3	28				0				0
17	3	27	2				0	27	0	3	30				0
18	3	30	1	30	0	1	31				0				0
19	1	31	1	31	0	0	31				0				0
20	1	32	3				0				0	32	0	1	33
21	1	33	1	33	0	8	41				0				0
22	1	34	3				0				0	34	0	3	37
23	1	35	1	35	0	2	37				0				0
Total						3.64				0.00				0.00	

So how can the computer and information technology help us to make more effective decisions and enhance some of those environments in which healthcare professionals work? In healthcare settings, as in other educare professions, technological changes have brought about both improvements in practice and challenges. The healthcare worlds in which we work become more complex and turbulent. To practice in a safe and accountable manner reflection in and on action becomes essential. We need all the help we can get sometimes to try to make sense of what is happening around us. In the reflective practice literature we have the notions of critical friends and 'companions'. We have aids to learning from experience such as critical incident analysis and learning journals. Information technology can also be seen as an aid to learning from experience. Technology will continue to change and develop, demanding a technologically literate population, willing to embrace new methods of analysis (ways of seeing). The data contained in this chapter is included to show, if only briefly, what is possible. The aim is to illustrate how the computer can do much work for us and, in so doing, enable us to spend time reflecting on the results.

One of the positive things that I have tried to show here is that IT encourages the 'what if' frame of mind. I have taken a number of situations, thought about their essential elements and used the computer to 'play' with them. The key is not to become enslaved by the software. We need to know what the software package can do for us. This is often time-consuming but, in my experience, time often well worth investing. By 'playing' or 'manipulating' the variables, we can make the model more or less 'life-like'. We can say things like, 'well here I need to increase the consultation time...' and 'here I need to add in something else to make it more realistic'. At the end of the day the bottom line is an answer to the question, 'so what?'. There seems to be little merit for busy healthcare professionals to become bogged-down with the technicalities of the package. What we need is the appropriate skill-mix in our reflective teams (Ghaye and Lillyman, 2000) so that those who are computer literate help and support others either to input the data or perhaps more importantly interpret the results. Most colleagues are likely to be interested in the interpretation and discussion of results. For many this is where the action is, learning from the data, weighing up options in the light of this and planning future action. One of the most important attributes of reflective practices is to open up new possibilities for action, new ways of seeing and new sensitivities. I hope that the tables and figures in this chapter are a start in this direction.

An increasing number of courses for healthcare professionals involve the introduction of computers and the use of information technology. In schools because of the implementation of the national curriculum a more computer literate population is emerging. Students pursuing post school qualifications expect to use, and are expected to use, IT in the majority of their work, irrespective of subject discipline or vocational orientation. These will increasingly form part of our technologically aware population. These students (which of course include nursing students) are maturing with an expectation of using IT to enrich their learning and to use it as an aid to effective and efficient learning.

Arguably, it is those people already in employment that face the biggest challenge. They need to have similar expectations from IT. However, through lack of knowledge, a large proportion of these people still see IT as an 'add-on' to their decision-making and organisation. They need support, guidance and encouragement to fully embrace the technological opportunities available. Dean (1998) comments that 'the inclusion of technology and technological innovations should be another tool to aid the planning of individualised patient care'. The arguments for the increasing use of technology in analysis and planning are strong but rely on a working knowledge of information technology 'without feeling intimidated by the computer' (Ashworth, 1990; Mann, 1992). Healthcare professionals need to rise to this challenge — our children, the patients of tomorrow, are depending on them.

References

Ghaye T, Lillyman S (2000) *Reflection: Principles and Practice for Healthcare Professionals.* Quay Books, Mark Allen Publishing Ltd, Dinton, Salisbury, Wiltshire

Lighthill J (ed) (1978) *Newer Users of Mathematics.* Penguin Books, London: 249–259

Rothery A (1990) *Modelling with Spreadsheets.* Chartwell-Bratt Publishing, London:1–6, 47–60

Recommended reading

Ashworth P (1990) High technology and humanity for intensive care. *Intensive Care Nurs* **6**: 150–160

Dean B (1998) Reflections on technology: increasing the science but diminishing the art of nursing? *Accid Emerg Nurs* **6**: 200–206

Dennis TL, Dennis LB (1991) *Management Science.* West Publishing, California: 544–627

Mann R (1992) Preserving humanity in an age of technology. *Intensive Crit Care Nurs* **8**: 54–59

Nickerson RC (1998) *Business Information Systems.* Addison-Wesley Educational Publishers, Massachusetts: 231–239

9

When caring is not enough

Tony Ghaye

In the first chapter of the book I linked three ideas together. They were reflection-on-practice, the meanings of the term discourse and story. In that chapter I said that the caring moments in this book might usefully be seen as stories of experience. In this sense they are value-laden stories. They have also been stories told mainly through a qualitative medium. But in *Chapter 8* we used numbers to make the point that we can develop a storyline in very different ways. In ways other than in words alone. *Chapter 8* also serves to make the point that we all have preferred ways of creating a story. Creating it with numbers and words is not everyone's preferred way, but arguably a very important one with the developing healthcare technologies in the new millennium. In this book we have not exploited poetic, visual, musical, still and video forms (Prosser, 1998), 3D modelling and other art-based forms (Pratt and Wood, 1998), verbal and non-verbal processes, concept mapping and so on. We have suggested that we need the courage to explore them as all of these can, for certain individuals and groups, be important catalysts to help make sense of practice. They are mediums through which we can express ourselves and something with which we can work and engage. We have also made the point that the story that is produced as well as the process of story-making and telling are important. Additionally and in the first book in this series (Ghaye and Lillyman, 2000a), we learnt that merely having experience is not enough. What counts is what we do with it. In *Caring Moments: The discourse of reflective practice* we hope that we have shown what can be done with experience set out in a story form. Learning through reflection is paramount here.

A number of things might usefully be considered by those wishing to engage in reflective writing of the kind presented in this book. I have set these out below. It takes the ideas I sketched out in *Chapter 1* a little further forward.

Creating a caring moment

Finding something significant to write about

This is more easily said than done. Practice is often so complex that it is difficult to disentangle one thing to focus upon. Alas and all too frequently, the focus becomes that part of our work that we feel less happy about, that needs 'fixing' and fast. This has got reflection a bad name. While it is understandable that many of us reflect on things like this, reflective practice is not only about putting right the things that are perceived to be wrong! This is a serious danger. We should also spend some time reflecting on the good bits, the things we are pleased about, right now. If we fail to do this, what is good and right today may become less attractive tomorrow. The reason for this is simple. We work within a dynamic and fast changing healthcare system. Therefore we cannot confidently assume that good today will be good tomorrow. Conversely, some less good and worrying things of today can become less significant and worrying in tomorrow's world. When creating a caring moment (a story) to learn from, we should consider at least two basic kinds, stories-of-celebration and stories-of-reconstruction. Both are stories that need to be created and should be heard. Both are stories that precipitate action, but action of different kinds. The first requires the kind of action that tries to nurture, preserve and nourish all that is good in that particular caring moment. The second requires that kind of action that has to try to improve (reconstruct) the existing situation as depicted in the story. Simply writing down a caring moment is not enough. Caring moments require us to act. Caring alone is not enough.

Allowing ourselves to be creative

Creating a caring moment is, (or can be) as the phrase suggests, a creative experience. In one way this can be described as moving from something known (or something we claim to know) that is to say the chosen aspect of practice, to something as yet unknown (practice re-told in story form). For most people 'being creative' can bring with it some anxiety. But this need not necessarily get in the way especially if you find yourself working with a skilled reflective practice facilitator.

Resist being stifled by conventions

Storying can be stifled by literary conventions. In my experience some healthcare workers are more preoccupied with this than with seeing storying essentially as a process of communication and learning. They worry more about their spellings, sentence construction, about writing in the first person, using 'I' and 'we' than anything else! I am often asked 'do you really want me to write it like an essay?' For some, these are real anxieties. They are anxieties that often touch upon some deep-seated and pervasive difficulties about writing, about how to write and about positioning ourselves clearly within our own story. In this sense they have to be respected. Conventions are important. They need to be understood and used, but in the appropriate context.

Place the emphasis on communication

What we say and how we say it, matter. Arguably creating a caring moment reflects a desire to discern and assign meaning to our work. So it is understandable that we might ask the question, 'what makes a "good" caring moment?' They might have the following qualities. I have deliberately stated each one in a positive manner. A caring moment is,

* **Recountable**: This means that a chosen practice event (significant incident) can be identified and reasons given for its choice. That the events in the incident can be presented in some way and put in some kind of sequence to form a storyline. We may recount alone or co-write. This is where storying becomes a collaborative experience.

* **Told in a particular way**: Not only do choices have to be made about what is told but also about how the story is communicated. It may be done amusingly, angrily, sarcastically, provocatively, suspiciously, confidently, hesitantly and so on. 'Stories are important only as told' (Cohler, 1991, p.182). We may tell them to ourselves and/or to others. We may read our story out aloud, on our own, or in a group (to an audience) and with the help of others. We may draw upon some other mediums (see above) to help us tell our story. I would argue that the use of caring moments in helping us reflect-on-practice

(therefore learning from them and trying to move forward) requires an 'optimistic orientation'. This means that by telling the story we give ourselves a chance of adding meaning to our lives, of establishing our 'preferred story' and through persistence and curiosity, seeking out and constructing an 'alternative story'.

* **Followable**: A good story is one that can be followed. This is often a complex task and not as straightforward as it might sound. We may claim our story is 'followable'. Others may disagree. Striving to make ourselves understood seems rational and logical. But many of us can never claim that we know ourselves in a complete, coherent and uncomplicated way. We have many 'selves', not one self. We have fragmented stories to tell, not fully knowable ones. We often have to strive to make connections. These are often not clearly apparent. We need to work out the difference and the links between the extra-ordinary (exceptional) and the ordinary. For a story to be followable it needs to have some kind of coherence about it. Sometimes this is not easy to establish. I am also making an assumption that the story-teller actually wants their listener/s (audience) to follow their story.

* **Likely to affect its audience**: This is also a tricky quality with a number of parts. In presenting our caring moment (telling our story) we need to have some idea of the effect we are trying to create, or it might create, with its audience. However, 'If one's self-image depends upon how others react, it seems natural that narrators would want their audiences to understand and agree with them. Therefore most storytellers emphasise only those experiences and reasons that their audiences find plausible' (Rosenwald and Wiersma, 1983; Tolman, 1991), 'they tell their stories in genres that their audiences are likely to recognise' (Harding, 1992; Modell, 1992) and 'they explain away whatever their audiences might find inappropriate' (Ochberg, 2000, p.110). The caring moments that we choose to recount and communicate do not just fill us (the audience) in on clinical events. They should not be seen merely as people telling us about themselves and what they have done. The act of telling can also be seen as a way the teller tries to create a relationship (of a particular kind)

with the audience. But I said this was a tricky quality. The assumption I am making is that talking through a caring moment might be seen as a way of 'making connections' (with practice, with other colleagues, with the audience and so on). It might also be seen as a way of keeping us at bay. Language and the way we use it can do this. This dual quality of 'inviting the listener in' but also of 'pushing the listener away' is important to understand, especially in the context of clinical supervision (Ghaye and Lillyman, 2000b). We should not accept the simple idea that everyone tries to make their story 'followable'. Some who present their story may not expect or even want their audiences to understand them. They may not wish their audience to understand them in the same way as they claim to understand themselves. They may think it foolish or inappropriate to present a clear and transparent story, particularly if they have any kind of doubts about the motives of the audience. But there is also something else that touches upon the connected qualities of a caring moment being 'followable' and affecting the audience.

* **Likely to affect the story teller**: We have tried to stress through the books in this series that reflection, of one kind or another, done in particular ways can be upsetting, 'dangerous' and unleash a torrent of frightening feelings that can be overwhelming for those who are participating. Reflective practices may well be important, but it is important that they are done well. On the other hand reflective practices, such as storying, can be therapeutic and emancipating. I am describing strong feelings here. For some the reflective experience then may be regarded as a cathartic one. Reflection can unlock human potential.

Give the therapeutic, emancipatory and empowering effects of storytelling a chance

The therapeutic benefits of storytelling were noted in the nursing literature more than 60 years ago (Bacon, 1933). More recently Banks-Wallace (1998) in discussing the emancipatory potential of storytelling in a group, (which she called 'Sisters in Session') outlined six possibilities. These were that storytelling helped to provide,

* **Contextual grounding**: The story provides a context that helps to position or locate ourselves in the world. The context influences how we see ourselves and others, the choices we make and how we act. The context is like the canvas and frame upon which we paint a picture of practice.

* **Bonding**: In her research with women of African descent living in the Seattle-Tacoma region of the USA, she claims that bonding with other group members was the most important function of storytelling.

* **Validation and affirmation**: The stories that were shared and the reactions of the group (audience) were an important means of women validating themselves and their reality. 'Validation of negative aspects often was a prerequisite to being able to critically examine their lives and make decisions regarding necessary changes. Stories affirming joy and goodness... were uplifting and energising' (p 20).

* **Venting and catharsis**: Using storytelling to vent emotions was important to the group. 'No one ever really talked about the "heaviness" of the topics being discussed. There were only a few times when someone cried... Many cathartic stories focused on the pain and frustration associated with living in the US as a woman and person of African descent' (p 20).

* **Storytelling as an act of resistence**: This is the role stories can play in exposing, challenging and confronting dominant structures, discourses, myths and stereotypes. It is a way that, through the stories we tell, we can resist and critique the dominant storylines. These may be the storylines that come from males, medics, management, government ministers and so on.

* **Education**: The communication of caring moments (stories) can, over time, be a way of creating a special kind of practical wisdom. This is eloquently described by Tschudin,

Telling stories is essential in reflective practice. What is important, however, is that we listen to the essence of what the person is saying rather than to what we want to hear. The patient who says, 'I am scared of this operation' is not heard if she gets an answer like, 'You'll be alright; this sort of operation is routine here and you have a good surgeon'. The patient needs to tell her story of fear: what the fear is, when it started, why it started and where it has led her. In stories of human suffering, we need to hear not so much the practical details as the untold and perhaps not yet understood meaning. In doing this, we are carrying out the essential work of any ethic: being receptive, relating to the other and responding in the most fitting way. In listening to others, we are sharing and expressing that we are 'with' them. In sharing, we become equal, and this allows us to be moral (1999, pp. 14–15).

Caring moments are value-laden moments. Creating caring moments reflects our use of two kinds of values. Our espoused values (what we say we do in our work) and our values-in-action (what we actually do). These are often not congruent. We say one thing and then end up actually doing something else. Sometimes we are not good at living out our values in our practice. So, creating a caring moment is not enough. Telling the story and listening respectfully to it, is not enough. Acting upon it in some appropriate way, might be. Just saying that we care is not enough. We have to act in a manner congruent with our espoused caring values. In short, we have to be prepared to learn something from each caring moment that is recounted to us. This might be about ourselves, about each other, our patients and clients, about treatments, the contexts in which our practice takes place and many other things.

Hopefully this book has shown that creating and reflecting on each caring moment is not like trying to repair a faulty machine. Creating a caring moment, telling, listening and learning from it, is not finding out what has gone wrong and then setting about trying to repair it. The whole exercise is not about correcting deficits, inadequacies and malfunctions within us, the team we may be a part of and the organisation for whom we work. The process should be viewed more positively and optimistically than this. Creating and reflecting on 'caring moments' should be undertaken with patience, persistence, deliberation and delicacy. The learning that may arise from reflective practices, of one kind or another, needs to be given the chance to breathe and emerge. This might usefully be done in the spirit of 'co-exploration' (Monk *et al*, 1997).

References

Bacon F (1933) Getting well with books. *Am J Nurs* **33**(11): 1143–1146

Banks-Wallace J (1998) Emancipatory potential of storytelling in a group. *Image J Nurs Sch* **30**(1): 17–21

Cohler B (1991) The life story and the study of resilience and response to adversity. *J of Narrative and Life History* **1**(2–3): 169–200

Ghaye T, Lillyman S (2000a) *Reflection: Principles and Practice for Healthcare Professionals.* Quay Books, Mark Allen Publishing Ltd, Dinton, Salisbury, Wiltshire

Ghaye T, Lillyman S (eds) (2000b) *Effective Clinical Supervision: The role of reflection.* Quay Books, Mark Allen Publishing Ltd, Dinton, Salisbury, Wiltshire

Harding S (1992) The afterlife of stories: Genesis of a man of God. In: Rosenwald G, Ochberg R (eds) *Storied Lives.* Yale University Press, New Haven

Modell J (1992) Work, identity and narrative. In: Rosenwald G, Ochberg, R (eds) *Storied Lives.* Yale University Press, New Haven

Monk G *et al* (1997) *Narrative Therapy in Practice: The Archaeology of Hope.* Jossey-Bass, California

Ochberg R (2000) On being part of an audience. In: Moch S, Gates M (eds) *The Researcher Experience in Qualitative Research.* Sage Publications, London

Pratt M, Wood M (eds) (1998) *Art Therapy in Palliative Care: The Creative Response.* Routledge, London

Prosser J (ed) (1998) *Image-based Research: A Sourcebook for Qualitative Researchers.* The Falmer Press, London

Rosenwald G, Wiersma J (1983) Women, Career Changes and the New Self. *Psychiatry* **46**: 213–229

Tolman D (1991) Adolescent Girls, women and sexuality: Discerning dilemmas of desire. In: Gilligan C, Rogers A, Tolman D (eds) *Women: girls and psychotherapy.* Harrington Park, New York

Tschudin V (1999) *Nurses Matter: Reclaiming our professional identity.* Macmillan, Basingstoke

Index